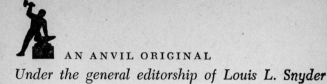

AN ANVIL ORIGINAL

Under the general editorship of Louis L. Snyder

THE AGE
OF REASON

LOUIS L. SNYDER

Professor of History
The City University of New York

VAN NOSTRAND REINHOLD COMPANY
NEW YORK CINCINNATI TORONTO
LONDON MELBOURNE

To
MICHAEL and VERA KRAUS
and MRS. EDELSTADT

Van Nostrand Reinhold Company Regional Offices:
Cincinnati, New York, Chicago, Millbrae, Dallas

Van Nostrand Reinhold Company International Offices:
London, Toronto, Melbourne

Copyright © 1955 by Louis L. Snyder

Library of Congress Catalog Card Number 55-6235

Manufactured in the United States of America

Published by Van Nostrand Reinhold Company
450 West 33rd Street, New York, N.Y. 10001

Published simultaneously in Canada by
D. Van Nostrand Company (Canada), Ltd.

30 29 28 27 26 25 24 23 22 21 20 19 18

PREFACE

The eighteenth-century Age of Reason was a crucial period in the formation of the mind of modern liberal man. The thinkers of the Enlightenment labored to free the intellect from the fantastic myths and fanaticisms that had enslaved it for centuries. Liberalism, tolerance, humanitarianism, natural law, the social contract, the social sciences—these are some of the fruits of a great period in human history.

The Age of Reason is one of those "big" topics that generally is undercut in the classroom in order to complete a course in Modern European History. Because of space limitations, even our mammoth textbooks can afford to devote only a small section to this most important subject. The student is faced with a choice of reading highly detailed monographs or of delving into many great books of the period to find the essentials of their contributions.

This volume is designed as that "something extra" needed to clarify the Enlightenment for the busy student and layman. At the same time, the unessential is eliminated. After considering the general characteristics of the Age of Reason, this Anvil Book treats the mechanical interpretation of nature, and in successive sections it shows how the idea of natural law was applied to religion, society, and government. Concluding chapters deal with the rise of modern experimental sciences, literature in the Enlightenment, and art and music. Part II gives readings from the great books of the period, selected in each case to illustrate the points in the text. Explanatory introductions are designed to place each selection into proper focus.

Louis L. Snyder

TABLE OF CONTENTS

Part I

THE ENLIGHTENMENT:
AGE OF FAITH IN SCIENCE

— 1 —

GENERAL CHARACTERISTICS OF THE AGE OF REASON

Meaning and Chronology. The Age of Reason, known to German scholars as the *Aufklärung,* to some British historians as the Illumination, and now generally termed the Enlightenment, was a great intellectual revolution that gave the modern mind its temper and spirit. Modern man, rejecting medieval theology as the final authority, now sought to interpret the universe, the world, and himself in terms of reason or logical analysis. In contrast both to Renaissance humanism and the motivating ideas of the Reformation, the Age of Reason was an intellectual, rational movement, which substituted for the medieval Age of Faith an Age of Faith in science. For the first time since the Greeks, thinkers began to attack all sorts of problems with fewer preconceived notions and inhibitions based upon doctrine or dogma. Merely as a matter of convenience, the dates 1650 to 1800 may be assigned as the rough boundary marks of the Age of Reason. The new rationalism, first popularized in the seventeenth century, was widely considered by the eighteenth century to be the final key to the problems of mankind. During these two centuries, the rationalists, finding in mathematics what they believed to be an infallible method, accepted a mechanical interpretation of nature and constructed a world-machine to explain the secrets of nature. The contributions of Copernicus and Descartes led eventually to the application of natural law to religion, to society, and to government. Remarkable advances in science and technology,

resulting from a new spirit of inquiry and encouraged
by the opportunities of an expanding commerce, confirmed the rationalists in their faith.

Characteristics. Various characteristic strains may
be observed in the pattern of the Age of Reason:

1. *The Secularization of Learning:* Where medieval
philosophers and theologians interpreted the universe
and man in terms of the Scriptures, the rationalists
tended to avoid ecclesiastical authority and turned more
and more to the secularization of knowledge. The door
to understanding, they insisted, was not revelation, but
mathematics, reason, and logic. This did not necessarily
mean, they were careful to point out, that all facets of
religion must be rejected. They objected specifically to
supernaturalism, on the ground that it was an obstacle in
the path of tolerance, freedom, and scientific discovery.

2. *Faith in Reason:* The Age of Reason was an age
of faith in the rational behavior of nature and in immutable scientific laws. Reason, said the rationalists, was
the omnipotent arbiter of all things, a powerful and
beneficial guide superior to all traditional authority. Man
was destined, they said, to use his intellect in solving the
manifold mysteries of nature and his own mind.

3. *Utilitarianism:* The spirit of the Age of Reason was
utilitarian and practical. Human beings, said the rationalists, should promote their own happiness and welfare
by remaking their lives and institutions on this earth.
That which was useful was good. And men deserved the
blessings of life, liberty, and property.

4. *Optimism and Self-Confidence:* The rationalists
were supremely confident and optimistic men, fully convinced of their ability to discover natural laws and to
perfect the world and life in accordance with them.
Science was still in its early stages and there was much
to be learned, but these self-assured men were exalted by
their discovery of a new gospel for mankind. Even if
they were not wholly successful in their self-appointed
task of unlocking the secrets of nature, they, nevertheless, made gigantic strides in opening new fields of
knowledge.

Meaning of Rationalism. An understanding of the

Age of Reason hinges on the meaning of the term "rationalism." According to B. Groethuysen rationalism "is a comprehensive expression applied to various theoretical and practical tendencies which aim to interpret the universe purely in terms of thought, or which aim to regulate individual and social life in accordance with principles of reason and to eliminate as far as possible or to relegate to the background everything irrational." This means that reason is a source of knowledge in itself, superior to and independent of sense perceptions, opposed to sensationalism. The development of rationalism has a history of its own. The Greeks were the first people to attack irrationalism with an objective and contemplative rationalism. In the Roman world, reason, synthesized with will, became an instrument for the control of individual and political life. During the Middle Ages, as we shall see, confidence in the power of reason disappeared in medieval religion; it was revived in the Renaissance as traditional religious views began to disintegrate. In the seventeenth century reason was regarded as a compulsory sovereign force from above, based on the will of the state. In the eighteenth century reason was looked upon as the collective expression of free, enlightened individuals. Nineteenth-century romanticism claimed that there were social forces that could not be understood by the use of reason. In the twentieth century further emphasis was laid on the concept that even science is not always subject to rational human thought.

The belief of the rationalists in the eternal truths of reason gave direction to man's thinking since the eighteenth century. Crane Brinton tells us that the agents of the Enlightenment had no doubts about the validity of their series of leaps from the law of gravity to human relations:

> Reason applied to human relations will show us that kings are not fathers of their people, that if meat is good to eat on Thursdays it is good to eat on Fridays, that if pork is nourishing to a Gentile it is nourishing to a Jew. Reason will enable us to find human institutions, human relations that are "natural"; once we find such institutions, we shall conform

to them and be happy. Reason will clear up the mess
that superstition, revelation, faith (the devil of the
rationalists) have piled up here on earth.[1]

Medieval Climate of Opinion.   In the Middle Ages
the world was regarded simply as a portion of the Kingdom of God. All phenomena were believed to have been
caused by God's will, sometimes acting by obvious and
sometimes by inscrutable means. It was not deemed
necessary nor wise to investigate further into the causes
of natural phenomena. Interest in nature lay primarily
in its meaning in terms of God's purpose. Omniscient
and omnipotent God had created the world in six days.
Man himself had been created by God in perfect form,
but because of his disobedience in the Garden of Eden,
he had fallen from grace and had been condemned to
eternal damnation. Man had been redeemed by the
sacrifice of God's only son. Life on earth was merely a
temporary test for the human being. Eventually, the
earth would be destroyed by a great catastrophe. At this
time, a final separation would take place between good
and evil men, the latter being destined for eternal punishment and the former being transported to the Heavenly
City, where they would dwell forever in happiness. This
was the drama of human history. In the medieval
climate of opinion, man was expected to recognize his
rôle in this great drama, and, above all, to make no
unnecessary attempt to alter it.

Transformation of Attitude.   The gradual change
from this medieval conception of nature was hastened
by the needs and discoveries of an expanding commerce
and a new climate of opinion resulting from them. In the
transition from medievalism to modernity, new institutions arose—the sovereign national state, absolute monarchy, representative government, diverse Christian sects,
commercial capitalism, and a politically conscious bourgeoisie. Along with these new institutions came a distinct cultural transformation, reflecting the new age in
all its variegated designs. The new world required new
patterns of thought.

[1] Crane Brinton, *The Shaping of the Modern Mind* (New
York, 1953), p. 114.

The medieval thinker had turned to theology for answers to the problems of the universe and life; the rationalists preferred to rely on scientific investigation. Medieval scholars, dismayed by the multiplicity of things and events that seemed to defy logical interpretation, took refuge in broad theological concepts; the rationalists sought to ascertain truth by logic. Medieval scholars had been motivated by *ideas, concepts,* and *forms;* the rationalists turned to the consideration of *laws* and *functions.* The rationalists, dissatisfied with medieval hair-splitting, looked forward, not backward.

Contrast with Other Revolutions. The Age of Reason differed in character from all previous and subsequent intellectual revolutions. The Greek philosophers often descended into skepticism, whereas the rationalists, considered as a group, saw no limit to their ability to ascertain the truth. The humanists of the Renaissance, while strongly influenced by classical freedom of inquiry, were more interested in man himself than in nature. They attacked the old barren scholasticism because of its continued emphasis upon theology, but they paid only passing attention to the natural laws that attracted the interest of the rationalists. During the Reformation, the agents of the various Protestant sects substituted for the old medieval orthodoxy their own national types of dogma, and sought for absolute, revealed truth in the Bible. The rationalists, on the other hand, turned away from revelation, and attempted deliberately to change existing institutions, traditions, and standards.

Search for an Infallible Method. During the course of the Age of Reason, European intellectuals cast off their narrow provincialism in favor of cosmopolitanism and humanitarianism. What was the key to the secrets of the universe? What were the infallible methods for solving the persistent problems of mankind? The early rationalists, seeking for natural laws, discovered the magic key in mathematics. Then came an intensive effort to "mathematicize the universe." Subsequently, other rationalists applied the methods of rationalism to religion, society, and government, on the assumption that human behavior could be explained on the basis of universal principles. The man of the Enlightenment attempted to shape life rationally on the basis of his own will.

A Word of Caution.   Despite the seemingly radical break with the past, the rationalists were nearer the Middle Ages and less emancipated than they thought. Carl Becker, in his *The Heavenly City of the Eighteenth-Century Philosophers*, offers a word of caution: "If we examine the foundations of their faith, we find that at every turn the *philosophes* betray their debt to medieval thought without being aware of it. They denounced Christian philosophy, but rather too much, after the manner of those who are but half emancipated from the 'superstitions' they scorn. They had put off the fear of God, but maintained a respectful attitude toward the Deity. They ridiculed the idea that the universe had been created in six days, but still believed it to be a beautifully articulated machine designed by the Supreme Being according to a rational plan as an abiding place for mankind. . . . They renounced the authority of church and Bible, but exhibited a naive faith in the authority of nature and reason. They scorned metaphysics, but were proud to be called philosophers. They dismantled heaven, somewhat prematurely it seems, since they retained their faith in the immortality of the soul. They courageously discussed atheism, but not before the servants. They defended toleration valiantly, but could with difficulty tolerate priests. They denied that miracles ever happened, but believed in the perfectibility of the human race. In spite of their rationalism and their humane sympathies, in spite of their aversion to hocus-pocus and enthusiasm and dim perspectives, in spite of their eager skepticism . . . there is more of Christian philosophy in the writings of the *philosophes* than has yet been dreamt of in our histories." [2]

Weaknesses of the Enlightenment.   Carl Becker's brilliant passage serves as a corrective for the assumption that the Age of Reason represented the high water mark of civilization. Like all men, the rationalists had their weaknesses. They had an exaggerated belief in the per-

[2] Carl Becker, *The Heavenly City of the Eighteenth-Century Philosophers* (New Haven, Conn., 1932), pp. 30-31.

fectibility of man, a blissful state that had not been attained by the pagan Greeks with their accumulated wisdom nor by Christianity in two millennia of its existence. Yet, the agents of reason assumed as a matter of course that man could attain a state of perfection on earth if only their precepts were followed with religious intensity. It was a monumental simplification. Reduced to black and white in the Rousseauan sense, what was natural was good, what was unnatural was evil. All men had to do was to understand natural law and regulate their actions accordingly. If they used their minds to control themselves and their environment, they would be on the road to true happiness. They failed to see that between black and white are subtle shades of gray.

Added to this was a fervent belief in the progress of man. Condorcet went so far as to formulate a decalogue of progress in his *Progrès de l'esprit humain,* in which he showed how man progressed from savagery to the edge of perfection on earth. Neither Condorcet nor Vico, nor their fellow rationalists, went on to explain the mystic force that lifted man from one level to another (it remained for the nineteenth-century Darwinian social evolutionists to come up with one explanation). The danger in this simplified analysis of human development was in an inordinate emphasis upon the material side of human progress. Progress came to mean a zealous search for better bath-tubs and more efficient mouse-traps. The physical and biological sciences have given us the discovery of atomic energy and the development of biological warfare—giant strides in material progress. The uses to which these innovations may be put have dismayed and alarmed the entire civilized world. How much more fruitful would be the application of reason to cope with this grave new world!

A Fundamental Change in Human Thought. Despite these weaknesses, the Age of Reason was one of the few movements in history that resulted in an important, new outlook upon existence and prepared the way for new and untried ways of future development. Granted that the rationalists could not purge themselves altogether of the old provincial outlook upon life, they did succeed in opening a new dynamic world perspective. They were responsible for the formation of a new climate of opinion, in which the accepted systems of belief and conduct could be challenged, both orally and by the written word. It was the rationalists' emphasis upon freedom of expression that drove from the minds of men the crippling fear of being burned at the stake. Their regard for the natural rights of the individual was something novel and precious in human history. Above all, the rationalists taught us that reason has always conquered those who try to restrict or abolish it. The attempt has been made again and again to throttle human reason; again and again it has failed.

The decisive historical character and mission of the Age of Reason was expressed by Kant in a famous passage in his *Response to the Question: What Is Enlightenment?* (1784): "Enlightenment is the liberation of man from his self-caused state of minority. Minority is the incapacity of using one's understanding without the direction of another. This state of minority is self-caused when its source lies not in a lack of understanding but in a lack of determination and courage to use it without the assistance of another. *Sapere aude!* Dare to use your own understanding! is thus the motto of the Enlightenment." In response to this appeal, not only philosophers and scientists, but aristocrats and professors, writers and publicists, bankers and amateur scholars, preachers and absolute monarchs, all began to seek more knowledge about the physical universe. Throughout human society there arose a hopeful belief in the steady improvement and ultimate perfection of mankind, through the use of reason and more knowledge of natural law. This was, indeed, an extraordinary change in the story of man's journey on earth.

Implications: The Open Society. Within the context of the intellectual traditions and social structure of the modern West, the Age of Reason represented a movement for a more open society—the pursuit of individual happiness, the security of individual liberties, constitutionalism, tolerance, cosmopolitanism, the unfettering of thought, and a society of free citizens based on law. Rationalism was the intellectual side of a politico-economic pattern, in which the secularized bourgeoisie abandoned in fact and in theory the universal, imperial concept of the medieval world and supported vital changes in the political and social order, such as democracy and liberalism. The open society of the West, stemming from the Age of Reason, placed great reliance on the autonomy of the individual, on voluntary association, and the rational and humanitarian regard for one's fellow man.

The Closed Society. This may be compared with historical motivations in Germany, Russia, and the Near East, where the socio-political order was not changed essentially by the intellectual trends of the Age of Reason. Here a politically vague universalism persisted, and the tendency was towards an authoritarian uniformity of state and faith. Where the rationalism of the West exalted the individual, the East stressed collective power and the state. While the West was impressed by the social contract and the universal similarities of nations, the East turned to the irrational folk-concept—the myth of the blood and the idea of inferior and superior nations. The West appealed to individual rights, the East to collective rights. The West was optimistic on the possibilities of natural law; the East lacked self-assurance and relegated the individual citizen to the position of a lackey of the state. Small wonder, then, that the East, rejecting the ideas of the Enlightenment, developed authoritarian, closed societies.

Pattern of Change. The Age of Reason represents no single school of thought and no systematic program. It was both theoretical and practical in its aspirations; it was concerned with philosophical analysis as well as the techniques of politics. We shall see, however, that the general pattern can be identified and that its unity of purpose had a decisive effect on the course of subsequent historical development. The Age of Reason was responsible for freeing the minds of men from centuries of myths and fanaticisms. It set the standard for our contemporary ideal of an objective, coöperative social science.

"The special effort of the Enlightenment," says Charles Frankel, "was to find a foundation in every field, from the profane sciences to revelation, from music to morals, and theology to commerce, such that thinking and action could be made independent of speculative metaphysics and supernatural revelation. Religion was treated mainly as an appendage to morals and discussed as though it were a part of physics. History was written to place European life in balanced perspective among other ways of life, none of which enjoyed the special sanction of God. In politics, the conception of divine right and supernatural providence were replaced by 'the social contract,' so that governments could be evaluated as instruments of human desire. In moral philosophy the effort was to base moral codes on Natural Law or on the 'well-established facts' of human psychology. In general, the eighteenth century attempted to bring together two secular traditions which had not always been in sympathy with each other—humanism and science. The classic humanistic persuasion that nothing human can be alien to a cultivated mind was given a spine and a positive program by the scientific demonstration of the reign of universal law. Erasmus had passed into Voltaire." [3]

[3] Charles Frankel, in *A History of Philosophical Systems,* ed. by Vergilius Ferm (New York, 1950), p. 267.

2

FROM FIXED COSMOS TO LIMITLESS UNIVERSE: THE MECHANICAL INTERPRETATION OF NATURE

The Ptolemaic System. Astronomy, the science of the celestial bodies, first took shape in Babylonia, where, in the third millennium B.C., the first measurements were made of the heavens and many of the constellations were named. Greek and Roman philosophers fashioned astronomy into a coherent science. From their point of view, the earth was located at the center of a number of transparent spheres, on which were fixed planets and stars, some turning clockwise, others counter-clockwise. These early efforts to grapple with the problem of celestial movements culminated in the work of Claudius Ptolemy, a celebrated Alexandrian mathematician and astronomer, who lived in Egypt in the second century A.D. In his famous *Almagest,* Ptolemy projected the geocentric theory, holding that the earth is an immovable sphere, fixed in the center of the universe. The sphere of the heavens revolves around the earth from east to west, carrying all celestial objects with it, once in every twenty-four hours. In order to explain the shifting position of the planets, Ptolemy advocated an epicyclical theory of planetary movement, holding that the planets move in smaller circles on the surface of their spheres.

Medieval Astronomy. Although they regarded the Ptolemaic System as a pagan theory, theologians of the Middle Ages accepted it because it harmonized well with appearances and seemed correct to the senses. Indeed, the whole logic of theology rested on a geocentric view of the universe. Obviously, the earth had to be the center of the universe, since it had to be important enough to

serve as an abode for the people of God before they left
it for the next world. To the theological mind, the circular motion of the planets and stars was an indication of
the endless spirit of eternity.

Copernicus: Explorer in the Cosmos.   The man who
proved the solar system to be heliocentric (sun-centered)
was a Polish astronomer, Nicholas Copernicus, who was
born in Thorn in 1473. In 1510 he became canon of
Frauenberg, dividing his time between his religious
duties, the practice of medicine, and astronomical studies. Absorbed in these occupations, he projected an entirely new system of astronomy, resulting in a fundamental change in man's conception of the universe. In
1507 he began work on a great astronomical treatise, De
Revolutionibus Orbium Coelestium, which he completed
in 1530. The work was not published until 1543, when
the first copy reached the author as he lay on his death-
bed. Copernicus died unaware of the fact that the preface he had written in dedicating the book to Pope Paul
III had been marred by the inclusion of an anonymous
section seeking to disarm the reader by calling the
treatise purely hypothetical in character.

Dissolution of the Firmament.   The Copernican
thesis was revolutionary in its implications. It exchanged
the positions of the sun and the earth in the scheme of
crystalline spheres. According to Copernicus, the sun
remains stationary, while the planets, including the earth,
revolve around it. In effect, this was a daring revolt
against the dictatorship of Ptolemy. Copernicus relied in
part upon ancient Greek astronomical knowledge and in
part on discoveries made in the fourteenth and fifteenth
centuries, but he was the first modern astronomer to
give scientific expression to the heliocentric theory.
Astronomy was now recast on an inverted design. The
first powerful argument was given for the existence of a
harmonious order of the universe. "I found," wrote
Copernicus in his preface, "after careful investigation
extending through years, that if the movements of the
other planets were referred to the motion of the earth in
its orbit and reckoned according to the revolution of
each star, not only could their observed phenomena be
logically explained, but also the succession of the stars,

and their size, and all their orbits, and the heavens themselves would present such a harmonized order that no
single part could be changed without disarranging the
others and the whole universe."

The Earth Shrinks. The Copernican proposition,
one of the great achievements of human thought, won
its way only slowly to acceptance as truth. It meant a
revolutionary change in man's attitude towards the whole
universe and even towards himself. It swept him from
his position as the central figure in the universe and
made of him "a tiny speck on a third-rate planet revolv-
ing around a tenth-rate sun drifting in an endless cosmic
ocean." This was a dangerous challenge to theologians.
In denying that the earth was the center of the universe,
the Copernican theory contradicted the doctrine that the
earth as well as the universe were created to serve the
needs of man. Both Catholic and Protestant theologians
condemned the Copernican theory as absurd. The Vati-
can officially pronounced it to be "false and altogether
opposed to Holy Scripture." From 1616 to 1757, the
De Revolutionibus was listed on the Index as being sub-
versive of truth. Not until 1822 was this ban lifted, and
the sun was given formal sanction to become the center
of the planetary system. Despite the unfavorable circumstances surrounding its appearance, the Copernican
theory gradually won recognition. It was an epoch-
making achievement, marking the end of the whole
system of medieval science.

Elaboration: Bruno. The Copernican theory was
elaborated and popularized by an Italian philosopher,
Giordano Bruno (c. 1548-1600). Despite his magnificent
achievement, Copernicus understood little about astro-
physical relativity and the plurality of worlds and universes. Although he had overthrown Ptolemy's geocentric
universe, Copernicus saw fit to retain its system of
spheres and epicycles. Some important gaps in the
Copernican system were filled in by Bruno on the basis
of brilliant intuitions, later confirmed: 1. there is neither
a center nor a limit to the universe, since everything is
relative to the point of observation; 2. there are other
universes besides our own; and 3. there are no fixed
starry spheres, since the heavenly bodies move freely in

space. These conclusions are all the more remarkable when it is considered that they were made in the period of pre-telescopic observation.

A disdainful, boastful, arrogant individualist, Bruno had little patience with those who disagreed with him. His attempts to popularize the Copernican theory and his scoffing attitude towards Aristotelian astronomy drew upon him the wrath of the Church. He was told that his hypothesis of the plurality of worlds and universes was in direct contradiction to the account of the Creation in Genesis. Accused of challenging the basic principles of Christianity, disturbing the belief of communicants, and stimulating heretical thoughts, he contemptuously dismissed the charges as nonsense. He was doubly suspected because he had been a Dominican in his early years, and had been forced to flee from Italy because of his heretical views on transubstantiation. Wandering through Europe, he spoke loudly against religion in general, placing it on a level with Greek myths. Daring to return to Venice, he was arrested by emissaries of the Inquisition in 1593, brought to Rome, and imprisoned for seven years. Finally, he was excommunicated and burned at the stake in 1600. The first human to sense the infinity of the universe, Bruno became the first martyr of the new science.

Pre-Telescopic Observation: Tycho Brahe. The Copernican system was more simple than the Ptolemaic. It soon became obvious, however, that a really decisive test between the two theories could not be made until observations of greater accuracy were recorded and made available to scientists. This was realized through the work of a Danish scholar, Tycho Brahe (1546-1601), who, although not altogether convinced of the validity of the Copernican theory, nevertheless contributed to its final acceptance. Constructing one of the best astronomical observatories of his time, the Castle of Heaven, on an island between Denmark and Sweden, Tycho Brahe located scores of stars, prepared the most useful stellar charts of his day, and, in general, perfected the art of pre-telescopic observation. He used plain sights placed far apart on a large mural quadrant, from which he was able to observe the heavenly bodies and measure their positions. With consummate skill he devised a number of other instruments with which he was able to achieve an unprecedented degree of accuracy. It was typical of the spirit of the times that Tycho Brahe was honored in his day more as an astrologer than as an astronomer.

Planetary Motion: Kepler. Tycho Brahe's young German assistant, Johann Kepler (1571-1630), a young man of unlimited imagination, was not altogether satisfied with his duties of observation and record-keeping. He became fully familiar with the vast body of material gathered in the great observatory. Untiring and patient, he evaluated, compared, and calculated the data at his disposal. By applying to his work a great theoretical talent, as well as a mastery of mathematics, he effected a major revolution in astronomy, and, indeed, may be called the founder of modern physical astronomy. Although a convinced Copernican, he, nevertheless, was destined to destroy a part of the Copernician order, namely, the system of fixed crystalline spheres that were supposed to control the motion of the heavenly bodies. Originally, he had accepted the traditional belief that all celestial revolutions must be performed in fixed circles, but after laborious computations he came to the conclusion that the planets traveled freely in space around elliptical orbits. This was, in effect, the basis for a new cosmic system, which Kepler expressed in three laws of planetary motion:

1. The planet describes an ellipse around the sun in one focus.
2. The radius vector drawn from the sun to the planet describes equal areas in equal times (*i.e.,* the planet moves fastest when nearest the sun).
3. The squares of the periodic times (*i.e.,* their times of revolution) of the several planets are proportional to the cubes of their respective mean distances from the sun.

The third law was announced by Kepler in an extraordinary book, *De Harmonice Mundi* (*On the Harmonies of the World*), which appeared in 1619. Kepler recounted his intense belief in the idea of an underlying harmony in nature, and gave an extensive mathematical analysis to prove it. His discoveries resulted in the perfection of a mathematical plan of the solar system as well as an enhancement of the predicting powers of astronomy. Not only did Kepler explode the old Aristotelian and Ptolemaic conceptions of planetary motion, but he also showed the way to future astronomers to find the cause as well as the mode of planetary motion. With Kepler the old idea of a hierarchy of being, approaching perfection as it receded from the center of the earth (an idea expressed in beautifully rolling syllables by Dante), gave way to a uniform mathematical law. Kepler made it plain that experiment was not only possible but necessary in the task of explaining the cosmos.

The Star-Gazer: Galileo. Mathematics as the only key to unshakable knowledge was the paramount discovery of the sixteenth century, but it remained for an Italian astronomer and experimental physicist, Galileo Galilei (1564-1642), to give it practical and convincing application. Galileo was a mathematical and mechanical genius from the days of his youth. Born in Pisa, the son of a well-known mathematician, he constructed mechanical toys when still but a child. As a student at the University of Pisa, he made one of his most important discoveries—the law of vibrations or swings of a pendulum. He also invented the hydrostatic balance as a means of ascertaining the specific gravity of solid bodies. In 1588 he obtained a professorship at the University of Pisa, where he propounded the theorem that all falling bodies descend with equal velocity. According to legend, he is said to have proven his point by several experiments conducted from the famous Leaning Tower. Driven from Pisa in 1591 by the Aristotelians, whose enmity he had incurred by his experiments, he went to the University of Padua, where he attracted students from all over Europe. Here he invented a thermometer, a proportional compass, and a microscope.

By far the most important of Galileo's inventions was his telescope, which he modeled on that of Hans Lippershey of Middleburg in Holland. His telescope enabled Galileo to make many important advances in astronomy. In 1610 he discovered four of Jupiter's satellites, which revolved around the planet as the moon revolves around the earth. He demonstrated the uneven configurations on the surface of the moon, and calculated the height of the mountains on it. He contemptuously dismissed the prevalent notion that the spots on the moon were the stains of Adam's sins, and, instead, stated that they were simply valleys. He described the Milky Way as a great collection of stars, and he detected sun-spots, from which he inferred the rotation of the sun.

In his *Sidereal Messenger,* first published in 1610, Galileo gave a dramatic account of his first telescopic observations. He described how a report reached his ears some ten months previously that a Dutchman had constructed a telescope, with the aid of which visible objects, although at a great distance from the observer, could be seen distinctly. Some proofs of its wonderful performance were recorded, to which some persons gave credence, while others refused to believe it. A few days later, Galileo received confirmation of the report in a letter from Paris written by a French nobleman, Jacques Badovere, which finally determined him to inquire into the principle of the telescope. After intensive studies, mainly on the theories of refraction, he succeeded in inventing a similar instrument. He prepared a tube, made of lead, on the ends of which he fitted two glass lenses, both plane on one side, but on the other side one spherically convex, and the other concave. Bringing his eyes to the concave lens, he saw objects large and near—larger than when they were to be seen with the natural eye alone. A little later, he constructed another telescope, which magnified objects to an even greater extent. At length, by sparing neither labor nor expense, he succeeded in making a superior instrument of greatly increased power. His first telescope magnified three diameters; a later one eight diameters; and finally one magnified thirty-three diameters.

"Without paying attention to the use of the telescope for terrestrial objects," Galileo wrote, "I betook myself to observation of the heavenly bodies; and first of all I viewed the moon as near as if it were scarcely two semidiameters of the earth distant. After the moon, I frequently observed other heavenly bodies, both fixed stars and planets, with incredible delight."

Galileo's experimental confirmation of the Copernican

theory on the constitution of the universe and his sarcas-
tic attacks upon those who persisted in their reverence
for Aristotle led him into difficulties with the Church.
His work was found to be at odds with passages from
the Scriptures. He replied with an exposition of a formal
theory on the relation of physical science to Holy Writ,
embodied in his book, *The Authority of Scripture*
(1614). As a sincere Catholic, Galileo was genuinely
interested in reconciling Copernican theory with orthodoxy: "It is surely harmful to souls," he wrote, "to
make it a heresy to believe what is proved. The prohibi-
tion of astronomy would be an open contempt of a
hundred texts of the Holy Scriptures, which teach us
that the glory and the greatness of Almighty God are
admirably discerned in all His works, and divinely read
in the open book of the universe." Here was indication
that, although Galileo's work led him in directions that
could easily be construed as away from the Scriptures,
he himself felt that his observations and experimentation
merely added light to the greatness of God and the
magnificent universe.

Ecclesiastical authorities felt otherwise. Galileo was
warned by the Inquisition against holding, teaching, or
defending Copernicus's theory, which had been placed
on the Index in 1616 "until it should be corrected." The
position of the Church was stated flatly: "The doctrine
that the sun is the center of the world is false and
absurd, formally heretical and contrary to Scripture,
whereas the doctrine that the earth is not the center of
the world but moves, and has further a daily motion, is
philosophically false and absurd and theologically at
least erroneous."

Although he promised to obey this injunction, Galileo
in 1632, ignoring his pledge, published his *Dialogue on
the System of the World,* which gave the Ptolemaic
theory its death-blow. He continued his attacks on the
Aristotelians: "The number of thick skulls is infinite,
and we need neither record their follies nor endeavor to
interest them in subtle and sublime ideas. No demonstrations can enlighten stupid brains. . . . I affirm that
the center of the celestial convolutions of the five planets
—Saturn, Jupiter, Mars, Venus, and Mercury, and like-

wise of the earth—is the sun. As for the moon, it goes round the earth, and yet does not cease to go round the sun with the earth."

Galileo was again summoned before the Inquisition. After a long and wearisome trial, he was sentenced to incarceration at the pleasure of the court, condemned to abjure on his knees by oath the truth of his scientific beliefs, and enjoined to recite penitential psalms once a week for three years. Legend has it that, once outside the courtroom, the irrepressible astronomer, after carefully noting that no one was looking, shook his fist in the general direction of the courtroom and shouted *"Eppur si muove"* ("It moves, all the same"). Even if this story be untrue, surely Galileo must have said so in the retreat of his mechanical mind.

Early in his career Galileo had accepted the traditional cosmology, but after reading Kepler he was persuaded to join the ranks of the Copernicans. His discoveries eventually confirmed and gave tangible expression to the Copernican theory. He made his work easily intelligible to the general public, thus popularizing a theory which until his time had made an impression only upon a relatively small group of scholars. It is most unfortunate that Galileo and Kepler ignored each other's work in the field of planetary motion. Had they been able to work together it is possible that Galileo's practical dynamic mechanics and Kepler's generalizations would have resulted in an earlier discovery of the force of gravitation. As it was, both these great intellects paved the way for the Newtonian synthesis.

Scientific Methodology: Francis Bacon. Among the apostles of the new inductive, experimental method, none was more influential than the illustrious Francis Bacon (1561-1626), philosopher, lawyer, essayist, and Lord Chancellor of England. During an active and successful public career, Bacon never lost sight of a dominant passion—to revolutionize philosophy by turning its material from speculative metaphysics to experimental science. In three remarkable books, *Novum Organum, Advancement of Learning,* and *New Atlantis,* he astutely attacked the deductive method of scholasticism and with great eloquence described the line of march of the new scientific methodology. An enthusiastic herald of modern science, he repudiated the traditional authority in favor of experimentation. He warned that the man of science must center his interest on the laboratory not the cathedral. In setting forth the widening intellectual breach separating the men of his day from the Middle Ages, he helped formulate a new conception of the universe and contributed much to the triumph of the mechanical interpretation of nature.

Bacon's procedure was to cleanse the Augean stables first by applying destructive criticism to all forces opposing acceptance of the new knowledge. In his *Novum Organum,* he warned that four *Idola,* or obstacles to clear-thinking, idols of the Tribe, Den, Market, and Theatre, had to be removed in order to insure against error in the collection of facts. (*See Reading No. 1.*) After exposing the obstacles to thinking, Bacon went on to suggest ways of overcoming them. He rejected traditional dogmas and individual prejudices, directed the thought of man to the study of the particular, and shifted the emphasis from arguments to facts. Experience, he said, is the only medium through which we may know things. The new science was strongly influenced by Bacon's classical formula: "Man, who is the servant and interpreter of nature, can act and understand no further than he has observed, either in operation or in contemplation, of the method and order of nature."

Language of Mathematics: Descartes. While Galileo confined himself to the study of mathematical and astronomical phenomena, his contemporary, René Descartes (1596-1650), a French philosopher and mathematician, began to describe in clear-cut terms the full outline of the new universe discovered by the rationalists. When still a young man, Descartes became deeply dissatisfied with the scholasticism that still survived in the teachings of the Jesuits from whom he received his early training. A Catholic who never quarreled with the official custodians of religious tradition, he, nevertheless, was alienated by the barren formalism of medieval scholasticism, and he was determined "to gain knowledge only from himself and the great book of the world, from nature and the observation of man."

Descartes wrote some of his books in French and others in Latin for a wide circle of educated readers. The procedure he proposed for the discovery of truth was first presented to the world in 1637 in his *Discourse on Method*, accompanied by three scientific treatises on geometry, optics, and general physics. In this work he projected four major principles he believed should be utilized for achieving the best results in philosophic and scientific study. (*See Reading No. 2.*) Utilizing these principles as his platform, Descartes went on to show that all phenomena, from the lowest form of life to the universe itself, functioned like a machine. Man, too, is a machine, differing from other animals in that he possesses consciousness. According to Descartes, the first principle in philosophy is to be found in individual consciousness: *Cogito ergo sum* ("I think, therefore I am"), an expression of the inseparable connection between consciousness and existence. He was conservative in religious matters: "You can substitute 'the mathematical order of nature' for 'God' whenever I use the latter term."

Descartes was one of history's great pioneers in the discipline of mathematics. Speculating on mechanical problems, he came to the conclusion that the source of all true science lies in a combination of geometrical analysis and algebra. He was the founder of analytical geometry—the application of algebra to geometry. "I saw," he said, "that there must be some general science to explain that element as a whole which gives rise to problems about order and measurement, restricted as these are to no special subject matter. This, I perceived, was called universal mathematics." So certain was he of finding an explanation for all things in purely mechanical terms that he boasted: "Give me extension and motion, and I will construct the universe!" He went on to invent a system of notation, the classification of curves, and a geometric interpretation of negative quantities, all of which have survived to the present day. His conception and systematization of the language of mathematics enabled the scientists who followed him to express their conclusions with greater accuracy and clarity.

In thus recognizing that mathematics constituted the

fundamental basis of physical science, Descartes laid
the groundwork for that exactness of observation and
calculation that was to become the outstanding characteristic of modern science. His work is considered of
such importance that it is generally recognized by the
term, the Cartesian Revolution. The old Aristotelian idea
that nature consists of a variety of unrelated objects,
each seeking to fulfil its aim in its own way, was now
superseded by the Cartesian principle that nothing in
nature is accidental nor arbitrary, but that everything is
governed by universal mathematical laws. Cartesianism
became the official beacon of the new science, even if its
explanations were as yet a little too simple and not
always proved by experimentation. Most important of
all, it effectively prepared the way for the great synthesis
of Newton, who has been called the greatest of the
Cartesians.

Harmonizer of the Universe: Newton. The triumph
of the mechanical interpretation of nature may be attributed to Isaac Newton (1642-1727), an English
natural philosopher. According to the French mathematician Legrange, Newton was "the greatest genius
that ever existed and the most fortunate, for we cannot
find more than once a system of the world to establish."
"The law of gravitation," wrote William Whewell, "is
indisputable and incomparably the greatest scientific discovery ever made, whether we look at the advance which
it involved, the extent of the truth disclosed, or the
fundamental nature of this truth." Lord Macaulay stated
"in no other mind have the demonstrative faculty and
the inductive faculty co-existed in such supreme excellence and perfect harmony." Newton himself was
unaffected by this extravagant praise, regarding himself
only "like a boy playing on the sea-shore, and diverting
myself in now and then finding a smoother pebble and a
prettier shell than ordinary, whilst the great ocean of
truth lay undiscovered before me."

Newton's genius became apparent in his early years.
He made his first experiment as a young man of sixteen
when a great storm raged over England. To find out the
force of the wind, he first jumped with and then against

it, and by comparing these distances with the extent of his jumps on a calm day, he was able to compute the force of the storm. In his early twenties he invented the binomial theorem, the method of tangents, and fluxional calculus. Late in 1665, according to Voltaire, the fall of an apple in a garden started Newton on a train of thought leading him to the discovery of universal gravitation.

Recognizing the validity of Galileo's law of falling bodies and Kepler's three laws of planetary motion, Newton synthesized and combined them in his own law of universal gravitation. He described his great discovery in his *Philosophiae Naturalis Principia Mathematica,* published as a whole in 1687. The planets revolve around the sun in harmony with Galileo's law of falling bodies. From one of Kepler's laws, namely, the proportionality of the areas to the times of their description, Newton inferred that the force that retained the planet in its orbit was always directed to the sun. From another one of Kepler's laws, namely, that every planet describes an ellipse around the sun in one focus, Newton drew the more general inference that the force by which the planet moves around the focus varies inversely as the square of the distance therefrom. He demonstrated that a planet acted upon by such a force could not move in any other curve than a conic section. Moreover, this force of attracting existed even in the smallest particle of matter. From all this he outlined the universal law of gravitation— *"Every particle of matter is attracted by or gravitates to every other particle of matter with a force inversely proportional to the squares of their distances."*

Newton's successful identification of terrestrial gravitation with the mutual attraction of the planets was the result of accurate mathematical comparisons. His great contribution was demonstrating the mechanical consequences of gravitation throughout the whole solar system. He showed gravitation to be the basic factor governing the movements of the planets. He explained the figure of the rotating earth by its action on the minuter particles of matter. He demonstrated how the

tides and the precision of the equinoxes worked on
the same principle. Finally, he accounted for some of
the more striking lunar and planetary inequalities.

Newton's account in his *Principia* of how he arrived
at the law of gravitation gives an excellent indication of
the rationalist's mind at work. In the past, he said, we
have sought to explain the phenomena of the heavens
and the seas by the power of gravity, but we have not as
yet been able to assign the cause of this power. Certainly, it must proceed from a cause that penetrates to
the very center of the suns and planets, without suffering
the least diminution of its force. It operates not according to the quantity of the surfaces of the particles
upon which it acts (as mechanical causes used to do),
but according to the quantity of the solid matter that
they contain. It extends to immense distances, decreasing
always in the duplicate proportions of the distances.
Gravitation towards the sun is made up out of the
gravitations towards the several particles of which the
body of the sun is composed. In receding from the sun,
gravitation decreases accurately in the duplicate proportion of the distances as far as Saturn.

Hitherto, Newton confessed, he had not been able to
discover the cause of those properties of gravity from
phenomena. "I frame no hypothesis; for whatever is not
deduced from the phenomena is to be called an hypothesis; and hypotheses, whether metaphysical or physical,
whether of occult qualities or mechanical, have no place
in experimental philosophy. In this philosophy particular
propositions are inferred from the phenomena, and
afterwards rendered general by induction. Thus it was
that the impenetrability, the mobility, and the impulsive
force of bodies, and the laws of motion and gravitation
were discovered. And to us it is enough that gravity does
really exist, and act according to the laws which we
have explained, and abundantly serves to account for
all the motions of the celestial bodies, and of our sea."
(*See Reading No. 3.*)

The crowning achievement of seventeenth century
science, Newton's law of gravitation, was another giant
stride forward after the revolutionary contributions of
Copernicus, Kepler, and Galileo. "If I have seen farther

than Descartes," said Newton modestly, "it is by standing on the shoulders of giants." Newton's magnificent
achievement was the construction of a world-machine;
instead of a series of planets, each going its own way
independent of all others, the universe now appeared
as a well-ordered, mechanical whole, held together by
gravity.

Natural Law Triumphant. Newton's law of gravitation marked the closing of an epoch in the history of
human thought and the beginning of a new era. The
nature of the cosmos as propounded by Aristotle, Ptolemy, and the medieval astrologers was overthrown and
placed in the category of outmoded knowledge. In its
place appeared a new cosmic theory of infinite scope and
complexity. The earth was demoted from its preëminent
plane and became only one tiny, relatively unimportant
planet in a maze of planets. The sun became just one
star in a system of thousands of millions of stars. The
entire system became one galaxy in a universe of thousands of millions of galaxies. Man was permanently
removed from his proud position at the center of creation
and was unceremoniously shoved into an inferior place.
He was now regarded as an infinitesimal organism, a
physical machine composed of atoms and molecules, and
governed by natural laws. But, as compensation, he was
rescued from a universe of chance and superstition and
given one of unfailing orderliness.

This—the orderliness of the universe—was the supreme discovery of science in the Age of Reason. Painstaking observations and calculations had proved that
celestial phenomena occur at regular sequences, often
complex, but always systematic and invariable. The
running of no clock ever approaches in precision the
motions of the heavenly bodies. To this day, clocks are
corrected and regulated by comparing them with the
apparent diurnal motions of the planets.

3

FROM REVELATION THROUGH DEISM TO MATERIALISM: APPLI-CATION OF THE IDEA OF NATURAL LAW TO RELIGION

Traditional Christianity. For more than seventeen hundred years Christianity had been constructing concepts of tradition, convention, and authority. The search was always for the perfectibility of man, which came only in a state of grace after death. The unity of the medieval Church was broken by the Protestant Revolt and the Catholic Counter-Reformation, together with the subsequent religious wars. Religious thought, however, had changed but little during these upheavals. Both Catholics and Protestants adhered tenaciously to their respective creeds and dogmas, and their religious disputes remained strongly emotional in character. The pattern remained much the same—the key to Christianity was revelation, the disclosure or communication of truth to man by God himself or by his authorized agents, the prophets and apostles.

Growth of Rationalism. The men of the Age of Reason thought it proper and wise to apply the findings of their conscious intellect to religion and to discuss it as though it were a part of the natural order. It was not only practical, they felt, but also highly desirable to consider religion as a pillar in the mechanical universe. The basis of religion, they said, was to be found not in revelation but in the very nature of man himself. Natural religion, they were certain, had always existed as a perfect thing, and revelation could add nothing to it. Miracles, prophecies, and religious rites were mere superstitions. This was, in essence, a new faith, a faith in the perfectibility of man on earth, in the future, to be sure, but *on earth*. These religious ideas of the Enlightenment, says Crane Brinton, whether they sprang from the head or the heart, were clearly corrosive of existing institutions. From the point of view of historical Christianity of the Middle Ages, the Age of Reason was a heresy, a distortion of Christianity. Newton and Locke set up two great ideas, Nature and Reason, which were to the Age of Reason "what such clusters of ideas as grace, salvation, and predestination were to traditional Christianity."

Dualism: Descartes. Among the first to apply the idea of natural law to religion was Descartes, whose rôle in devising the language of mathematics has already been discussed. Conservative in his approach, he sought to harmonize medieval thought with the new science by projecting a mechanistic universe in which everything could be explained by mathematics. From this mechanistic explanation he exempted two things—God and the soul of man, both of which he described as beyond and above science. He advocated a kind of philosophic dualism, by which God (or mind) and man (or nature) are distinct from one another. For anything to exist, said Descartes, although it be only an idea, there must be a cause whose reality and perfection is at least as great as the effect. The greater cannot proceed from the less. It follows that there must exist a being whose actual perfection is no less than Descartes' idea of perfection. Therefore, God exists.

Pantheism: Spinoza. Baruch Spinoza (1632-1677), a Portuguese-born Jew of Amsterdam, who was excommunicated by his synagogue for heretical views, was strongly influenced by Descartes but unwilling to accept his dualistic concept. In an era of voluptuous epicureanism, this pious, virtuous, God-intoxicated man lived the simple life of a lens polisher. Few human beings have ever been more maligned on the one hand and more venerated on the other than was this great genius. Scrupulously following the methods outlined by Descartes, Spinoza sought to create a mechanico-naturalistic philosophy of the universe. But he rejected Cartesian dualism and substituted for it the idea that God and the universe are one (pantheism). Spinoza saw God as the supreme and only real substance in the universe, the only object of true knowledge, an absolute and infinite Being. God as substance consists of infinite attributes, each expressing eternal and definite essence. "If this be denied," Spinoza said, "conceive, if it be possible, that God does not exist." It would follow, Spinoza reasoned, that His essence does not involve existence, which is absurd. Therefore, God necessarily exists. "God is absolutely the first cause. He acts from laws of His own nature only, and is compelled by no one. For outside of himself there can be nothing by which He may be determined to act. Therefore, He acts solely from the laws of His own nature. And, therefore, also God alone is a free cause." Spinoza denied that God is anthropomorphic (with human attributes), and insisted, instead, that He exists in all the various manifestations of mind and matter. God and nature are ultimately one and the same.

Contemporary Jews and Christians attacked Spinoza as an atheist and condemned his view of an all-embracing naturalistic God as impossible and heretical. The philosopher died a persecuted man. Today there is more inclination to recognize his attempt to combine devout mysticism and scientific axioms as an ingenious philosophic system. "For about a century," writes Abraham Wolf, "Spinoza's name was anathema. His writings were indeed studied and his ideas were borrowed to a greater extent than is commonly supposed. But people dared not mention his name with respect, much less acknowledge their indebtedness to him. In time, however, things improved. Lessing, Goethe, and Coleridge did most to rehabilitate his name, and others followed suit. The monument at The Hague, the *Spinozahuis* at Rijnsburg, and the *Domus Spinozana* in the Hague bear testimony to the reverence in which the memory of Spinoza is now held throughout the civilized world." (*See Reading No. 4.*)

Scientific Scholasticism: Leibniz. Another significant attempt to reconcile religion and science was made by Gottfried Wilhelm Freiherr von Leibniz (1646-1716), a German philosopher, mathematician, and versatile man of affairs. Where Descartes had separated things into two substances connected by the omnipotence of God, and where Spinoza had absorbed both into one divine substance, Leibniz rejected both, because, in his view, they were wrong in their understanding of substance. Substance, the ultimate reality, said Leibniz, can only be conceived of as a force. The universe is made up of an infinite number of individual centers of force, or *monads*. "The monads," he said, "are the very atoms of nature— in a word, the elements of things," but as centers of force, they have neither parts, extension, nor figure. This distinguishes monads from the atoms of Democritus and the materialists, for the former are metaphysical points, or spiritual beings, whose very nature it is to act. Each monad is a microcosm, throbbing with energy, the universe in little. From God there proceeds a continual emanation of monads. All monads, being independent of one another, are brought into rational organization through a predetermined harmony arranged by God. The "high grade" monads are souls. The soul of a human being is the dominant monad of the group that makes up his body, and unlike the inferior monads, acts purposively. Critics denounced these ideas as absurd.

It will be noted that Leibniz was a firm believer in God. To substantiate his belief, he borrowed available scholastic proofs of the existence of God, and, in effect, re-stated the old Augustinian philosophy in terms of mathematics and physics. He formulated a new scholasticism grounded on science. Where medieval theologians had drawn their data from religious texts, Leibniz turned to the impressive mathematical and scientific discoveries of his own century. His own original contribution to mathematics was the invention of infinitesimal calculus. His prime aim was to throw the light of reason on old theological concepts.

Conservative Rationalists. Descartes, Spinoza, and Leibniz may be called conservative rationalists, who, together with Isaac Newton, were convinced that religion must conform to reason and that their own version of religion did so conform. Others who were convinced that religion could be vindicated by rational analysis were John Tillotson (1630-1694), Archbishop of Canterbury; John Locke (1632-1704), the British philosopher; and Samuel Clarke (1675-1729), the foremost British

philosopher after Locke's death. These early advocates
of natural religion had a profound reverence for Holy
Writ, which they believed to be wholly consistent with
reason. Religion to them was an essential need of man.
God is the unquestioned ruler of the universe; a virtuous
life is necessary for all human beings; there is a future
life; and both the prophecies and miracles of the New
Testament are reasonable and logical. Religion is a science, like physics, and its truths can be ascertained by
logical analysis.

Deism: Religion of Reason. The conservative rationalists believed that natural religion is the foundation
of all revealed religion, but another group of rationalists,
the Deists, refused to compromise with the old mysticism, and established a new religion of reason. According to the Deists, God is an impersonal force, the cus-
todian of the world-machine and the clock-winder of the
universe. The God who fashioned the Newtonian world-
machine, they said, would never "reveal" anything to
man unless it were simple, clear-cut, and logical. Since
natural religion had always existed as a perfect thing,
revelation could add nothing to it. Admittedly, God had
created the universe, but once the work was done, immutable laws came into existence. It was useless and
presumptuous to attempt to change these laws by prayer
or by any other human means. The Deists accepted the
moral and ethical teachings of Christ, but they refused
to recognize the tenets of orthodox Christianity, which
they described as a mysterious and incomprehensible
body of revelation. They urged all creeds to follow four
precepts of natural religion: 1. God is to be regarded as
the master of the universe; 2. He asks only the good of
man, human perfection and happiness; 3. the aim of all
religion is virtue or decent living; and 4. men must rely
upon reason to solve their problems.

English Deism. The Deists were moderate religious
liberals standing midway between the conservative religious idealism of Newton and the atheism of d'Holbach. They represented an attitude, never an organized
sect. In England, a long line of Deists attacked, some
calmly and moderately, some vigorously, all that distinguished Christianity from natural religion. Lord Herbert

of Cherbury (1583-1648) announced his belief in the existence of God and in immortality, but rejected "all superstitious rites and doctrines." Charles Blount (1654-1693), the first popularizer of Deism in England, attacked miracles as fabrications, and ridiculed the sacramental system as a shameless, money-grubbing scheme. Matthew Tindal (c. 1653-1733) excoriated religious rites: "To imagine that God can command anything inconsistent with this universal benevolence is highly to dishonor Him; 'tis to destroy His impartial goodness, and make His power and wisdom degenerate into cruelty and craft." Thomas Morgan, who called himself a Christian Deist, maintained in his *Moral Philosopher* (1737) that Christianity was a revival of the religion of nature. Thomas Chubb (1697-1747) sought to make Deism palatable to the literate masses by contending that Christ was a true Deist. Anthony Collins (1676-1729) claimed that the fulfillment of prophecy by events in Christ's life was all "secondary, secret, allegorical, and mystical." Thomas Wollston (1669-1731) made a withering attack on the miracles recorded in the New Testament, calling them "foolish, trivial, contradictory, absurd, unworthy of a divinely commissioned teacher, and characteristic only of a sorcerer and wizard." For his pains he was imprisoned for blasphemy, and died in jail.

French Philosophes. The Deists' attacks on revelation and on Christianity in general were calm and moderate in England, but they were bitter and impassioned in France. The French *philosophes* considered themselves to be students of society whose task it was to enlighten mankind, sweep away the cobwebs of ancient superstitions, and let in the light of reason. The foremost propagandist of French Deism was François-Marie Arouet, known as Voltaire (1694-1778). Witty, erudite, and irascible, he utilized his pen to direct ridicule against Christianity, which he attacked as a system of absurdities. In his estimation, Christ was a religious fanatic, the Bible was the work of ignorant men, and miracles could be dismissed as simple falsehoods. "Every man of good sense," he scoffed, "every good man, ought to hold the Christian sect in horror. The great name of

Deist, which is not revered sufficiently, is the only name one ought to take. The only gospel one ought to read is the great book of Nature, written by the hand of God and sealed with His seal. The only religion that ought to be professed is the religion of worshipping God and being a good man." It will be noted that Voltaire, despite his attitude toward Christianity, did not regard himself as an atheist nor as a wrecker of religion. He observed that if there were no God it would be necessary to invent one. And it was impossible, he insisted, that Deism, "this pure and eternal religion," should produce evil. (*See Reading No. 5.*)

Voltaire's consummate controversial skill won him a reputation far beyond the borders of France. In his native land his chief rival was not to be found among his many imitators and followers, but in a famous set of books, the *Encyclopedia*. Like Voltaire, Denis Diderot (1713-1784), the leading French encyclopedist, satirized the obscurity of Christian doctrine, poked fun at the petty squabbles of priests and clergymen, and ridiculed the numerous sects of Christianity.

Jean-Jacques Rousseau (1712-1778) was more moderate in his religious views. Where Voltaire rejected both Christianity and Christ, Rousseau accepted both. The latter recommended that "one should regard in silence what cannot be disproved or comprehended, and one should humble one's self before the Supreme Being who alone knows the truth." He proposed, nevertheless, to establish Deism as the national civil religion. "The dogmas of civil religion," he said, "should be simple, few in number, announced with precision, without explanation or commentary. The existence of a powerful, intelligent, benevolent, prescient and providential divinity, the life to come, the happiness of the just, the punishment of the wicked, the sacredness of the social contract and the law—these are the positive dogmas."

German Deism. The attacks by the French Deists on Christianity presaged the intense anti-clericalism of the French Revolution. But where Deism may be accounted as a revolutionary movement in France, it took root only among a small group of intellectuals in Germany and the United States. Two leading German Deists were Hermann Samuel Reimarus (1694-1768), who denied the validity of miracles and maintained that natural religion was the absolute antithesis of revelation, and Gotthold Ephraim Lessing (1729-1781), who, although he praised "true Christianity," published extracts of Reimarus's works and thereby exposed himself to much petty persecution. The classic German expression of Deism was projected by Immanuel Kant (1724-1804), who supported the Deistic tenets of God, freedom, and immortality while defending religion unsupported by revelation. However, in stressing the needs of human nature rather than rational metaphysics, Kant helped prepare the way for the romantic philosophies of religion.

American Deism. Deism was transferred along with rationalistic political ideas to the American states, where Thomas Jefferson, John Adams, and Benjamin Franklin, among others, supported reason as the key to religion. The various threads of Deistic arguments were synthesized by Thomas Paine (1737-1809), propagandist for enlightenment and an important figure in both the American and French Revolutions. "I believe in one God and no more," Paine stated in his *The Age of Reason* (1796), "and I hope for happiness beyond this life. I believe in the equality of men, and I believe that religious duties consist in doing justice, loving mercy, and endeavoring to make our fellow-creatures happy. I do not believe in the creed professed by the Jewish Church, by the Roman Church, by the Greek Church, by the Turkish Church, by the Protestant Church, nor by any Church I know of. My mind is my own church. All national institutions of churches appear to me no other than human inventions set up to terrify and enslave mankind, and monopolize power and profit. . . . Each of these churches shows certain books which they call 'revelation,' or the word of God. . . . For my own part I disbelieve them all. . . . How different is this from the pure and simple profession of Deism. The true Deist has but one Deity, and his religion consists in contemplating the power, wisdom, and benignity of the Deity in His works, and in endeavoring to imitate Him in everything moral, scientific, and mechanical. . . .

The creation we behold is the real word of God, in
which we cannot be deceived. It proclaims His power, it
demonstrates His wisdom, it manifests His goodness and
benefices. The moral duty of man consists in imitating
the moral goodness and beneficence of God manifested
in the creation of all His creatures."

On one point, Paine concluded, all nations of the
earth and all religions agree—all believe in God. The
things in which they disagree are redundancies annexed
to that belief. Therefore, if ever a universal religion
should prevail, it will not believe anything new, but will
get rid of redundancies and will believe as man believed
at first. In the meantime, "let every man follow, as he
has a right to do, the religion and worship he prefers."
In the light of this explanation, it would seem that Theo-
dore Roosevelt's opinion of Paine as "that filthy little
atheist" was somewhat exaggerated.

American Deists in general tempered their opinions
because of political exigencies. American Deism as a
movement soon disappeared in the rising tide of evan-
gelicalism.

Defense of Christianity. The Deistic attacks upon
religion stimulated a spirited defense of Christianity. The
defense took the form of questioning the validity of
natural religion. William Law (1688-1761), an English
mystic, insisted that religion need not submit itself to
any test of reason. "A course of plain undeniable
miracles attesting the truth of a revelation," he said, "is
highest and utmost evidence of its coming from God,
and not to be tried by our judgments about the reason-
ableness or necessity of its doctrines." In his *The Case
of Reason, or Natural Religion Fairly Stated* (1732),
Law claimed that revealed religion is as worthy of belief
as natural religion. Either must one abandon religion or
abandon reason. In this case, Law said, the latter must
be rejected.

Bishop Butler's Two-Edged Sword. A strong attack upon Deism was made by Bishop Joseph Butler
(1692-1752) in his *The Analogy of Religion, Natural
and Revealed* (1737). Seeking to meet the Deists on their
own ground, Butler claimed that revealed religion, as well
as natural religion, could meet the tests of reason. Revela-

tion, he said, supplemented and did not contradict reason, though he admitted that its content could be comprehended only obscurely. He warned that it was impossible for true revelation to oppose the dictates of conscience, for both come from God. Using the analogy of a two-edged sword, Butler maintained that both natural and revealed religion form a unit and cannot be separated. The course of nature, with all its mysteries, inconsistencies, and imperfections, is just as incomprehensible to human reason as the so-called mysteries and injustices of the Scriptures. "Upon supposition that God exercises a moral government over the world, the analogy of His natural government suggests and makes it creditable that His moral government must be a scheme quite beyond our comprehension, and this affords a general answer against all objections made against the justice and goodness of it." Immortality, Butler continued, is reasonable; note the changes in man in his lifetime, such as the suspension of certain faculties during sleep. Admitting that the evidences of revealed religion do not amount to demonstration, Butler insisted that they were in the highest degree probable. (*See Reading No. 6.*)

It apparently did not occur to Bishop Butler that, in thus defending revealed religion, there might be those who would reject both natural and revealed religion as untenable. His great apology for religion helped lead to the rise of skepticism, although his arguments enjoyed a great vogue in English and American university circles, where it became a part of Christian apologetics.

Deism Evaluated. Deism as a religious movement was far too radical and unyielding for the Christian, and, at the same time, too conservative and compromising for the religious radical. It left a permanent residue in nineteenth and twentieth thought, particularly because of its emphasis upon religious toleration, its high regard for ethics, its attempts to harmonize religion with science, and its insistence upon regarding religion in the light of current intellectual and moral needs. Those who defended Deism praised it as a liberating influence in the emancipation of man from superstition and supernaturalism. Critics continued to regard it as a destructive force that attacked traditional beliefs and offered nothing of value in their place. The greatest weakness of Deism was its appeal limited to the educated upper classes. It made but little headway among the common people, who were repelled by its cold rationalism. It was easy to understand the simple precepts and the great ethical and moral lessons of traditional religion, but it was something else again to evaluate the harmonious and orderly Newtonian world-machine in terms of a religious belief.

Rise of Skepticism. The skeptics denounced Deism as too restrained and timid, and said that, like Christianity, it was beset by fallacies and inconsistencies. They were unwilling to acknowledge the existence of God, the truth of any religion, the divine origin of Christianity, or the validity of revelation. Thomas Hobbes (1588-1679), proclaimed to the heavens that he was a good Christian, and then proceeded to denounce religion as "accepted superstition," miracles as impossibilities, immortality as wishful thinking, and theological writing as "noise." "Religious and theological writings," he said, "fill our libraries and the world with their noise and uproar, but wherefrom the last thing we may expect is conviction."

Hume's Attack on Miracles. David Hume (1711-1776), Scottish philosopher and historian, ridiculed revelation and, at the same time, attacked natural religion. A confirmed skeptic, holding that God is unknowable, Hume insisted that the mind cannot comprehend God, because Absolute God cannot come into intimacy nor make Himself known to the finite mind. Hume's attack on miracles was bitter. He rejected the idea that miracles provided the supreme proof for Christianity. In his *Essay on Miracles* (1748), he stated flatly that no testimony is sufficient to establish a miracle, unless the testimony be of such a kind that its falsehood would be more miraculous than the fact which it endeavors to establish. "When anyone tells me," Hume wrote, "that he saw a dead man restored to life, I immediately consider with myself, whether it be more probable, that this person should either deceive or be deceived, or that the fact, which he relates should have happened. I weight the one miracle against the other; and according to the superior-ity, which I discover, I pronounce my decision, and always reject the greater miracle."

Hume denounced miracles as violations of the law of nature. He claimed that, since a firm and unalterable experience has established the laws of nature, the proof against a miracle, from the very nature of the fact, is as entire as any argument from experience can possibly be imagined. He pointed out that the many instances of forged miracles, prophecies, and supernatural events, which, in all ages, have either been detected by contrary evidence, or which detect themselves by their absurdity, prove sufficiently the strong propensity of mankind for the extraordinary and the marvelous. One ought reasonably, he concluded, to bear suspicions against all relations of this kind. "Upon the whole, then, it appears, that no testimony for any kind of a miracle has ever amounted to a probability, much less than a proof; and that, even supposing that it amounted to a proof, it would be opposed by another proof; derived from the very nature of the fact, which it would endeavor to establish. It is experience only, which gives authority to human testimony; and it is the same experience, which assures us of the laws of nature."

This was a recurrent theme in rationalist thought. For those who accepted the Newtonian conception of the universe, there could be no violation of the laws of nature. Whatever the cause of miracles (and Hume did not deny that they could take place), the clue was to be sought in natural law and not in revelation.

Kant's Critique of Pure Reason. Kant's *Critique of Pure Reason* (1781) is probably the most celebrated defense of agnosticism ever written. Kant felt that all arguments to prove the existence of God must, in order to be valid theoretically, start from specifically and exclusively sensible or phenomenal data, must employ only the conceptions of pure science, and must end with demonstrating in sensible experience and object congruous with, or corresponding to, the idea of God. But this requirement cannot be met, for, scientifically speaking, the existence of an absolutely necessary God cannot be either proved nor disproved. Kant thus rejected the old rational cosmology, theology, and psychology, all of which, he said, profess to attain a knowledge of super-phenomenal realities. He rejected rational theology, but in its place he sought to gain a more real and accessible faith springing from man's consciousness. While God cannot be known as First Cause and Architect of the Universe, we can and must believe in Him as a *moral* Governor. Man must seek, Kant advised, a high and austere morality, the true and basic function of religion.

Mechanistic Materialism: Atheism. The atheists categorically denied the existence of God. Holding that a completely mechanistic interpretation of man and the universe offered a correct explanation, they claimed that no further additions were necessary. They denounced religion as useful only to priests and politicians, and insisted that it was unnecessary as a means of improving man's moral and ethical conduct. Baron d'Holbach, a French chemist and philosopher of German origin, who settled in Paris, delivered powerful attacks on Christianity in his *System of Nature* (1770) and *Common Sense* (1772). There is nothing in the universe, he said, except matter in spontaneous movement. "Is it not more natural and more intelligible to derive everything which exists from the bosom of matter, whose existence is demonstrated by every one of our senses, whose effects we each instant experience, which we see acting, moving, communicating motion and generating ceaselessly, than to attribute the formation of things to an unknown force, to a spiritual being which cannot develop from its nature what it is not itself, and which, by the spiritual essence attributed to it is incapable of doing anything and of setting anything in motion?"

Holbach regarded religious feeling as a combination of superstitious fear and the desire to change unfavorable circumstances. Hence, he said, man believed in miracles and held that God might one day change the order of events to do man a favor. During droughts, men pray for rain. Holbach described God as naught but an exaggerated man, later spiritualized to absurdity. "The Jehovah of the Jews is a suspicious tyrant, who breathes nothing but blood, murder, carnage, and who demands that they nourish him with the vapors of animals. The Jupiter of the pagans is a lascivious monster. The Moloch of the Phoenicians is a cannibal; the pure mind of the Christians resolved, in order to appease his fury, to crucify his own son." Why, Holbach, asked, if God created man for his own glory, why does he not make himself known? And if God be good, why fear; if he be wise, why worry; if he be omniscient, why pray?

Holbach's greatest objection to religion was that, in his estimation, it held back scientific progress by a stranglehold on thinking. Under the instruction of the priests, he said, youth was shamefully sacrificed to superstition. From his infancy the child was poisoned by unintelligible notions, fed to him by mysteries and fables. The priests, Holbach said, filled the mind of the child with sophism and errors, intoxicated him with fanaticism, prepossessed him forever against reason and truth, and placed the energy of his soul forever under shackles.

In ridiculing his fellow-men for their religious beliefs, Holbach was seeking a simple solution for all the ills of mankind. With gusto and unshakable conviction, he presented his views in terms of black and white—there was knowledge (science, evidence) and there was ignorance (religion). Substitute knowledge for ignorance, he said, and the millennium would arrive. Reject religion, he said, and the mind of man would soar.

— 4 —

NATURAL LAW AND SOCIETY: THE SCIENCE OF MAN

Creation of the Social Sciences. Newtonian scientific method tended to have a destructive effect upon religious traditions, but it was responsible constructively for the creation of the modern social sciences. Distinct from such physical sciences as astronomy, physics, and chemistry, the social sciences may be defined as the mental or cultural sciences devoted to the study of human relationships. The Greeks, the first secular-minded people to become interested in man as man, made many valuable contributions to the understanding of social relationships, but they had too little scientific knowledge to establish a solid structure of the social sciences. Until the Age of Reason, Aristotle's and Plato's conception of political philosophy embraced all the social sciences. During the Middle Ages, the social sciences were superseded by theology, which regarded man's functioning in the group as important only so far as it affected salvation in the world to come.

The rationalists broke political philosophy down into its component elements. This, they believed, was their crowning glory. They sought for new laws to explain human institutions and behavior. They were certain that natural law could be applied to man and society as well as nature.

Scientific Materialism: Hobbes. Influenced by rapid advances in the mathematical and physical sciences, Thomas Hobbes (1588-1679), an English philosopher, attempted to construct a universal system of human knowledge that would explain man and society in the same manner as it explained natural phenomena. Accepting Newton's concept of a world in mechanical harmony and utilizing Descartes' language of mathematics, Hobbes sought to apply the new principles of mathematics and mechanics to mind as well as matter. Man, in both body and soul, he said, is an integral part of the natural order. The soul of man is not a spiritual substance distinct from matter, but is the result of the organization of matter in the body. It is possible, Hobbes said, to construct a science of human nature in the sense of a human physics. All that is needed is to observe and analyze the processes of thought in one's own mind; from these we can learn to know what the thoughts of other men are on like occasions.

Hobbes reasoned that man, in common with the rest

of the universe, was fashioned like a machine and functioned like one. He projected a theory of sensationalism,
according to which the fundamental element of human
life is to be found in matter in motion—the only reality
in the world outside of man's mind. "All that exists is
body (matter); all that occurs is motion." When this
motion comes into contact with man's sense-organs, certain sensations take place. All knowledge is derived from
these sensations. It follows that all positive knowledge
is the direct result of the impact of bodily particles on
sense organs. Hobbes believed that there is no conception in a man's mind, which has not at first, totally or by
parts, been begotten upon the organs of sense. The rest
are always derived from that original.

Empiricism: Locke. John Locke (1632-1704),
English philosopher, scientist, and physician, is generally
regarded as the founder of the school of empiricism,
which believes that knowledge comes only from sensory
experience. The knowing force, the "understanding,"
said Locke, can itself be understood only in terms of its
possible objects. In his *Essay Concerning Human Understanding* (1690), Locke popularized Hobbes' theory of
sensationalism. The extraordinary influence of this work
may be judged by the fact that it went through twenty
editions within ten years. According to Locke, the mind
at birth is a *tabula rasa,* a blank tablet, upon which all
sensations, and ultimately all thoughts, are written. The
materials of reason and knowledge spring from experience, upon which all knowledge is founded and from
which it ultimately derives itself. Our observation of
either external objects or about the operations of our
minds, perceived and reflected on by ourselves, is that
which supplies our understanding with all the materials
of thinking. These are the fountains of knowledge, from
which all the ideas we have, or can naturally have, do
spring. Here is the chain explaining how the human
mind became stocked with ideas: all knowledge begins
with the reception of sensations from without; these
sensations become images; these images, in turn, are
elaborated in a chain; and the chain becomes intelligible
thought. Once the understanding is stored with simple
ideas, it has the power to repeat, compare, and unite

them even to an almost infinite variety, and so we can make at will complex new ideas.

Locke went on to show that the mind, receiving ideas from without, turns its view inward on itself and observes its own actions about those ideas it has. The two great actions of the mind are perception (or thinking) and volition (or will). These two powers, or abilities, in the mind are called faculties. Some of the modes of these simple ideas of reflection are remembrance, discerning, reasoning, judging, knowledge, and faith. "It has pleased our wise Creator," Locke said, "to annex several objects, and to the ideas which we received from them, as also to several of our thoughts, a concomitant pleasure, and that in several objects to several degrees, that those faculties which He has endowed us with might not remain wholly idle and unemployed by us." The capacious mind of man, said Locke, can take its flight farther than the stars and cannot be confined by the limits of the world. It may often extend its thoughts beyond the utmost expansion of matter and make excursions into "that incomprehensible inane." (*See Reading No. 8.*)

Locke, in effect, was attacking Plato's doctrine of innate ideas, that is, that ideas are inherent in the human mind at birth. The struggle between those who advocate heredity and those who emphasize environmentalism as decisive in the human mind is one that has persisted among scientists to the present day. The importance of Locke in intellectual history is that, in demonstrating that knowledge should be based upon experience and reason, he literally created a new science of the human mind. His successors gave varied explanations of reality. George Berkeley (1685-1753), an Irish metaphysician, argued that the immediate objects of sight are all mind-dependent appearances, and that there is no material universe outside that reality that exists only in the mind. He gave the ultimate and final answer: *Substance is what it is experienced as.* In his *Principles of Human Knowledge* (1710), Berkeley held it to be self-evident truth that all those bodies that compose the fabric of the world have no real subsistence unless perceived by the senses. (*See Reading No. 9.*) David Hume, taking an extreme position on the sensationalism that was latent in Locke's account of the origin of knowledge, even went so far as to challenge the reality of the mind. Like Locke, he investigated the psycho-genetic origins of our ideas, insisting that the very notions underlying the experience-knowledge relation—self-cause, substance—these also demand analysis if we are to understand the nature of reality.

Equality: Helvétius. From the generalizations on sensationalism by Hobbes and Locke to the concept of the democratic ideal was but a short step. Claude Adrien Helvétius (1715-1771), a French reformer and idealist, believed that since all human beings at birth have exactly the same mind, and since all knowledge they acquire is the result of environmental influences, it must follow logically that all men must be equal at birth. He angrily rejected the idea that the masses are mentally inferior, arguing that they were intellectually just as capable as the upper classes, but simply lacked opportunity. "Who can be certain," he asked, "that a difference in education does not produce the difference observable in minds? Who can assert, that men are not like those trees of the same species, whose seed, being absolutely the same, but never sown in exactly the same earth, nor exposed entirely to the same winds, the same sun, or the same rain, must in unfolding themselves necessarily produce an infinity of different forms? I may then conclude, that the inequality observable in the mind of man may be indifferently considered, either as the effect of nature or of education."

Helvétius, on the basis of these views, insisted that equal educational opportunities for all classes were essential and reasonable. He described the art of education as placing young people in a set of circumstances fitted to develop in them the germs of intelligence and virtue. There would be a better society, he said, if reforming monarchs would recognize the equality of all men and grant them equal rights. He argued that freedom of the public press was absolutely necessary in civilized society, while complaining that "although most governments urge their citizens to search for truth, almost all governments punish them for finding it."

Helvétius was among the first rationalists to express the opinion that social progress was both possible and desirable. The medieval emphasis upon the future world and its description of the present world as an inferior and sinful place had left but little room for the fullness of joy on earth. The rationalists were more optimistic about the possibility of social progress. They felt that, while there had been but little biological change in man since ancient times, there has been remarkable progress in human learning. Each generation, they said, utilizes the intellectual possessions of its predecessors and adds its own achievements. The future of man lies in his own hands. He can use his brain to strive for perfection or he can work for his own destruction.

Law of Cycles: Vico. This idea of social progress was an impelling element in the work of Giovanni Battista Vico (1688-1744), an Italian jurist and philosopher, who utilized it in constructing his version of the story of civilization. Vico saw in the development of man the motivating power of a law of cycles—divine, heroic, and human, each successive stage higher than the preceding one. He described the history of humanity as a process of development from poetic wisdom—the impersonal, instinctive ideas of primitive society—to occult wisdom, which turns divinely implanted ideas into conscious philosophical wisdom.

Human Perfection: Condorcet. The most elaborate exposition of the idea of social progress was that made by the Marquis de Condorcet (1743-1794), a French philosopher, mathematician, and freethinker. In his *Outlines of an Historical View of the Progress of the Human Mind* (1794), Condorcet advanced the theory that the human race was continually advancing to perfection. He divided the history of mankind into nine epochs: 1. hunters and fishermen; 2. shepherds; 3. tillers of the soil; 4. commerce, science, and philosophy in Greece; 5. science and philosophy from Alexander to the decline of the Roman Empire; 6. the decadence of science to the Crusades; 7. from the Crusades to the invention of printing; 8. from the invention of printing to the philosophical revolution affected by Descartes; and 9. from Descartes to the Revolution of 1789, including the discoveries of Locke, Newton, and Rousseau, when reason, tolerance, and humanitarianism became the watchwords of man. In the tenth epoch—that of the future—man will progress to the point at which all inequalities of opportunity will be destroyed, and individual human nature will be perfected. The key factor in this progress will be popular education. (*See Reading No. 10.*)

Impact on Education. Sixteenth-century education was dominated by punitive mental and physical discipline. Preserved Smith tells the story of a Württemberg schoolmaster who carefully recorded that in a half century of teaching he had given 911,527 strokes with a stick, 124,000 lashes with a whip, 136,715 slaps with the hand, and 1,115,800 boxes on the ear. With the coming of the Age of Reason there was a strong revolt against this type of disciplinary teaching. Rationalism taught the virtues of destroying superstition and fears and of inculcating a spirit of tolerance and composure. The school, which had been a minor social agency in the past, influencing only a small minority of the population, began to expand in importance until, eventually, it took its place along with the state, the church, family, and property as one of the most powerful institutions in society.

The rationalists were deeply concerned with the problems of educational doctrine. Locke and Voltaire criticized the slavish pedantry of the classical school, but reserved their recommendations for the children of the wealthy, on the ground that little could be done to educate the masses. Rousseau and Helvétius, on the other hand, contributed to the democratization of education by insisting that education could remove handicaps faced by the masses. Rousseau praised the natural curiosity of all human beings, and urged the moulding of educational practice to the actual character of people. Condorcet, probably the outstanding advocate among the rationalists of popular education, advised equal opportunities in education for women, reflecting his conviction of the equality of the sexes.

In general, it may be said that in the Age of Reason a firm foundation was laid for the great educational revolution to take place in later times. The educational

theories presented by the rationalists were not actually
realized until the nineteenth and twentieth centuries,
when free public education became the order in all
civilized nations.

The New Political Economy. The application of
natural law to economics was expressed in the emergence of the science of political economy, with its own
new system of theories and symbols. The rising middle
class, driving to political and economic power, began to
see economics, like the universe, religion, and man, as
subject to natural law. It judged the older system of
mercantilism as outmoded. Mercantilism had been developed in Europe upon the decay of the medieval and
manorial systems; its policy was to secure a favorable
balance of trade, to develop agriculture and manufactures, to create a merchant marine, establish foreign
trade monopolies, and, above all, to keep commercial
enterprises under state control. By the middle of the
eighteenth century, the merchant and manufacturing
classes became so powerful that they began to resent any
interference by the state in their affairs and loudly
called for freedom of action. The middle class wanted
protection for its rights of property and contract, but, at
the same time, it insisted upon freedom from interference by the state. The idea of natural law provided a
perfect outlet for the demands of the manufacturing and
business entrepreneurs. A body of doctrine was devised
to assist the attack on mercantilism and to prove that
capitalism and natural law were in complete harmony.
Nature, it was said, meant the business man to be entirely free in his aim to obtain profits. Any attempt to
destroy that freedom was a violation of the laws of
nature.

Economic Liberalism: the Physiocrats. Economic
liberalism, extolling capitalism, individual liberty, and
natural law, was closely identified with the principle of
laissez faire ("let alone," or "hands off!"). It was
founded by a group of French physiocrats, who received
their name from a book written in 1767 by Dupont de
Nemours, *Physiocracy, or the Natural Constitution of
that Form of Government Most Advantageous to the
Human Race.* All human institutions—economic, social,

and political—said the physiocrats, are governed by natural law. They can be perfected only if they are made to conform to the natural order. Any legislative attempts to curb economic processes will violate natural law and lead to human unhappiness and misery. The government, in the physiocrats' view, should limit itself to the protection of life and property and to the promotion of public works and education. Private property, especially land, must be valued above everything else. Commerce and industry are of great utility to society, but they must be made subservient to agriculture. It was to the interest of all that restrictions on agriculture be removed, that there be complete freedom of cultivation, and that each individual be permitted to engage in free competition— "the mainspring of human perfectibility." Dupont de Nemours (1739-1817), François Quesnay (1694-1774), and Jean Vincent, Sieur de Gournay (1712-1759) presented an elaborate structure of physiocratic reasoning, all of which was given a practical application by Baron de Turgot (1727-1781).

Adam Smith's Wealth of Nations. Adam Smith (1723-1790), a Scottish philosopher, published his great work, *An Inquiry into the Nature and Causes of the Wealth of Nations,* in 1776. Smith's doctrines were not completely new; he took a mass of fragmentary ideas and arranged them into an organized system of economic thought. Instead of drawing conclusions from abstract principles, he observed the socio-economic facts around him and then sought to elicit their significance. He concluded that economic life is ordered to laws of nature. Mercantilism, he believed, arose from the mistaken theory that wealth consists in money. Once this theory had been established in general belief, it became the great object of political economy to diminish as much as possible the importation of foreign goods for home consumption and to increase as much as possible the exportation of the produce of domestic industry. This, according to Smith, was fallacious and evil. The contrivers of mercantilism had been the producers, not the consumers, whose interests had been entirely neglected.

If governments abstained from interference with free

competition, said Adam Smith, industrial and commercial problems would work themselves out and a practical maximum of efficiency in the economy would be reached. A maximum of wealth can be attained only by the unrestrained actions of individuals, for nature has seen to it that when each man seeks his own welfare he actually promotes the welfare of the nation. "Man's self-interest is God's providence." Unlike the physiocrats, who assigned primacy to agriculture because France was then a dominantly agricultural nation, Adam Smith exalted labor and not land as the main source of wealth. Rapid production, he said, depended largely upon a proper division of labor, whereby each member of society could perform his designated task efficiently and quickly.

Adam Smith shares with the physiocrats the honor of elevating political economy to a systematic examination of the processes of the production and distribution of wealth. While many of his important principles were superseded later, he did define clearly such economic concepts as division of labor, wages, profits, interest, and rent—terms that have since become commonplace. In discrediting the economic theories of the past, and, especially, in combining natural law and personal freedom, the *Wealth of Nations* became a convenient guide for social reconstruction. "The most valid element in Smith's work," wrote John Maurice Clark, "was his prescience in selecting for the emphasis accorded by a central formula those elements demanding fuller expression than the time accorded, and whose achievement of that fuller expression was destined to become the outstanding fact of a coming generation." Adam Smith's conclusions harmonized admirably with the aims and aspirations of a middle class delighted with his championing of the freedom of contract and with his attacks on "impertinent obstructions" and "the folly of human laws." (*See Reading No. 11.*)

The policy of economic freedom was beneficial when applied to business, but its effect on the workers was quite the opposite. Increasing industrialization led to widespread unemployment, poverty, and disease. Could it be possible that there were immutable natural laws making these conditions inevitable? Answers were given by Malthus and Ricardo, who have since received the distinction of having created the "dismal science" of *laissez faire*.

Law of Populations: Malthus. In 1798, Thomas Robert Malthus (1766-1834), an English clergyman and social philosopher, published anonymously the first edition of *An Essay on the Principle of Population*. This original version, written largely from memory and without substantiating material, aroused a storm of controversy. Malthus later published a second edition full of detail and abundantly documented. According to Malthus, population, when unchecked, increases in geometrical ratio (1,2,4,8,16,32. . . .), while subsistence increases only in arithmetical ratio (1,2,3,4,5. . . .). Population always hovers at the verge of the means of subsistence. It is prevented from going beyond this limit by the positive checks of war, famine, and pestilence, as well as by misery and vice. Since population is capable of doubling itself at least once in every twenty-five years, and since the supply of food can increase only in arithmetical ratio, it follows that the increase of population must always be checked by the lack of food. But, except in cases of famine, this check is never operative.

In spite of the checks of moral restraint, vice, and misery, Malthus went on to say, there is a constant tendency for population to increase beyond the means of subsistence. Such an increase is followed by lower wages, high prices, and a lower marriage and birth rate. The lower wages, in turn, induce more agricultural enterprise, whereby the means of subsistence become more abundant again. More plentiful and cheaper food then promotes marriage and increases the population, until again there is a shortage of food. This oscillation, although somewhat irregular, will always be found, and there will always be a tendency for the population to fluctuate around the food limit.

Malthus saw no way in which man could escape from the weight of this law, "which pervades all animated nature." He was profoundly pessimistic on the possibility for future progress of mankind. His critics claimed that:
1. he failed to foresee the great development of transport and colonization in the nineteenth century, as well as the

enormous increase in foodstuffs and raw materials; 2. he
did not understand that, while every addition to the
population meant another mouth to feed, it also gave
another pair of hands; and 3. he failed to see that the
rising standards of living in Western countries raised the
marriage age and lowered the birth rate. It has become
fashionable to disparage the Malthusian doctrine as out-
of-date. It should be added that the reading of Malthus's
essay suggested independently, first to Charles Darwin,
and then to Alfred Russel Wallace, the idea of natural
selection as a necessary consequence of the struggle for
existence. (*See Reading No. 12.*)

Iron Law of Wages: Ricardo. David Ricardo
(1772-1823), English economist, pamphleteer, banker,
and member of Parliament, had little sympathy for the
working class, which he regarded primarily as an instrument in the hands of successful entrepreneurs. He believed the misery of the workers to be inevitable and
permanent, a result of the unchangeable natural laws
governing human nature. There was an irreconcilable
antagonism, he said, between the three groups of the
community—landowners, capitalists, and wage-earners.
In his subsistence theory of wages, also called the iron
law of wages, Ricardo asserted that wages for the worker
always decline to a point where they provide him only
with the means of keeping body and soul together. "The
natural price of labor is that price which is necessary to
enable the laborers one with another to subsist and to
perpetuate their race without either increase or diminution." Since there is only a definite amount of wages for
the laborer, if one gets more than his share the rest will
suffer. The only solution is to render less frequent among
them early and improvident marriages. "There is no
means of improving the lot of the worker except by
limiting the number of his children. His destiny is in his
own hands. Every suggestion which does not tend to the
reduction in number of the working people is useless, to
say the least of it. All legislative interference must be
pernicious." If wages are raised, there must follow inevitably a lowering of profits, which is utterly wrong because it is opposed to natural law. (*See Reading No. 13.*)

Malthus was a benevolent clergyman and Ricardo was

considered an upright business man, but both came to exceedingly pessimistic conclusions. Both were convinced that poverty and misery were a part of God's natural order and that they were as natural as the rising of the sun. Critics denounced both the Malthusian and the Ricardoan doctrines because of their "incomplete data, defective methods, and misleading conclusions." But the contemporaries of the two implicitly believed in these ideas and consistently used them to resist any change. This was the tightly held dogma of the bourgeois entrepreneurs—if there were to be any adjustment of the miserable conditions of the working man, it had to take place as a consequence of the natural order. Man himself could do nothing.

— 5 —

FROM ABSOLUTISM TO POPULAR SOVEREIGNTY: NATURAL LAW AND GOVERNMENT

Theory of Natural Rights. We have seen how the rationalists applied the concept of natural law to celestial mechanics, religion, and economics. Some went a step further and used the methods of rationalism in the political field, constructing a body of theory, that, together with the profound socio-economic changing taking place in the eighteenth century, helped bring about the French Revolution. The efforts to rationalize political life on the basis of universal principles took two main directions. One school of thought, originating in the seventeenth century and continuing in the eighteenth, sought to justify absolutism in government as consonant with the laws of nature. The second, and by far the most important school, used scientific arguments in support of democracy and constitutionalism, tolerance, and popular sovereignty. From this school emerged the basic theory of natural rights of man.

Four Theories of Government. Four trends may be noted in eighteenth-century political science:

1. *The scientific argument in support of absolutism:* The idea of a scientific and enlightened despotism was defended in all Western Europe, with the exception of England, until the French Revolution.

2. *The scientific argument in support of constitutionalism:* The English concept of constitutionalism based on natural rights was popularized by the Frenchman, Montesquieu.

3. *The scientific argument in support of democracy:* The conclusion that democracy is by far the best of all possible political systems, since it is based on natural rights, was projected and popularized by Rousseau.

4. *The development of utilitarianism:* A rationalized exposition of socio-political problems, judging any scheme of society by its usefulness, was proposed by Jeremy Bentham.

Benevolent Absolutism. The idea of an enlightened, scientific despotism was promoted by a group of intellectuals who had little or no faith in the common man but a fervent belief in the sacred economic laws of property and security. Strongly opposed to *absolute* monarchy, which they regarded as an outworn vestige of earlier societies, they agreed to accept the political leadership of a monarch, provided that he showed due respect for the natural rights of man, *i.e.,* political, social, economic, and religious freedom. They were willing to tolerate such enlightened despots as Frederick the Great, Catherine II, and Joseph II, as long as these monarchs enforced the natural rights of the bourgeoisie. Thomas Hobbes approved the idea of absolute monarchy on the ground that the sovereign's formal judgment is the law of God and nature. This point of view was of little interest to the rising middle class, which saw ultimate sovereignty in itself and not in the person of the monarch. What the bourgeoisie wanted was a system of government that would protect it against the envy of the masses and the dominance of a powerful monarch.

Literary Weapon: The Encyclopedia. Among the most enthusiastic proponents of enlightened despotism were the Encyclopedists, whose work has already been mentioned. Diderot and Jean d'Alembert, perpetual secretary of the French Academy of Sciences, visualized the *Encyclopedia,* to which Voltaire, Montesquieu, Buffon, Quesnay, Rousseau, d'Holbach, and others contributed, as the first great attempt to create a positive synthesis of human knowledge. Its aim, according to Diderot, was "to gather together the knowledge scattered over the face of the earth, to set forth its general plan to the men with whom we live, and to transmit it to the men who will come after us." More precisely, its goal was to combat the older systems of thought based on tradition and authority, and substitute for them an edifice of knowledge based on science and reason. Perhaps no encyclopedia has been of such great political importance, for it sought not only to inform but to guide opinion. The organ of the most advanced and revolutionary opinions of the time, the manifesto of "the party of Reason and Humanity," it became an intellectual weapon and a proselytizing agency for free-thinking rationalists. Its execution was unequal, with excellent contributions mingled among loosely written articles. Much of its material was verbose, dogmatic, and inaccurate. Bitterly denounced by governmental, ecclesiastical authorities as the work of an organized band of conspirators against society, it was ridiculed as "chaos, nothingness, the Tower of Babel, a work of disorder and destruction, the gospel of Satan." But it was a mighty instrument in unifying the scattered ideas of the *philosophes* and in spreading their beliefs throughout Europe. Thousands of sets were published in France and translations were issued throughout Europe.

Anti-Despotism: Montesquieu. The leading theorist of anti-despotism was Charles Louis de Secondat, Baron de la Brède et de Montesquieu (1689-1755). Born near Bordeaux, Montesquieu was for ten years president of the Bordeaux court of justice. Interested in the philosophy

of law, rather than in administration, he traveled over
Europe to study the political and legal systems. For
twenty years he worked on his book *L'Esprit des lois*
(*The Spirit of the Laws*), published anonymously in
1748. In this book Montesquieu surveyed every political
system, ancient and modern, examined the principles and
defects of each one, and came to the conclusion that
English constitutionalism should be the model for all
countries. He postulated three types of government—
republican, monarchical, and despotic. Under a republic,
he said, the people, or a part of the people, have the
sovereign power. Under a monarchy, one man alone rules,
but by fixed and established laws. Under a despotism, a
single man, without law or regulation, impels everything
according to his will or caprice. Montesquieu indicated a
strong distaste for the latter form. Its requisite, he said,
was the prevalence of fear. From the nature of despotism,
a despot gives the government into the hands of another
man. "A creature whose five senses are always telling
him that he is everything and that other men are nothing
is naturally idle, ignorant, and pleasure-seeking." The
despot, therefore, abandons control of affairs. If he
entrusted them to several persons there would be disputes
among them, and the despot would be put to the trouble
of interfering in their intrigues. The easier way is for
him to surrender all administration to a vizier, to whom
he gives full power. The support of a vizier is a fundamental law of despotism. The more people a despot has
to govern, the less he thinks of governing them. The
greater the business of the state becomes, the less trouble
he takes to deliberate upon it. The despotic state continually grows corrupt because it is depraved in its
nature. Other forms of government perish through particular accidents, but a despotism dies inwardly, even
when accidental causes seem to support it.

Montesquieu contrasted this despotic state with the
popular state. In the latter the people are separated into
certain classes. The way in which this division is carried
out plays an important part in the duration of a democracy and its prosperity. Election by lot is a democratic
method of allowing every citizen a reasonable hope of
serving his country. But this is a defective measure, and

it is by regulating and correcting it that great legislators have distinguished themselves. The Athenian Solon, for example, projected a method of nominating by choice all the senators, judges, and military officers. It does not require much probity for a monarchy or a despotism to maintain itself, for the force of the laws in one, and the uplifted sword of the tyrant in the other, regulate and curb everything.

In a democracy, on the other hand, everything depends upon the political virtues of the people. When a democracy loses its patriotism, frugality, and passion for equality, it is soon destroyed. The principle of democracy may grow corrupt, not only when a people loses its spirit of equality, but also when this spirit of equality becomes excessive, with each man desiring to be the equal of those whom he has chosen to rule over him. Montesquieu warned against two excesses of democracy —the spirit of inequality, which leads to an aristocracy or to the government of one man, and the spirit of excessive equality, which ends in despotism.

Montesquieu was responsible more than any other intellectual figures of his century for the development of a unified science of human society. Sensitive to the delicate complexity of social organisms, he realized that an enormous amount of investigation was essential before any improvements could be made in legislation and government. His life was devoted to the accumulation of facts as a means of inferring concrete recommendations. He influenced his contemporaries by his championing of the right of remonstrance, his skilful thrusts at slavery, his denunciation of religious intolerance, his attack on primitive penal codes, and his eulogy of commerce as a stimulus to civilization. He prepared the foundations for nineteenth-century jurisprudence and sociology.

Montesquieu's great and enduring book not only stimulated the movement that culminated in the French Revolution, but it also induced those nations seeking for some golden mean between despotism and mob-rule to adopt the British parliamentary system. Curiously, he regarded British parliamentary institutions as an excellent example of the separation of three powers of government—judicial, executive, and legislative. Here he assumed something he wanted to find, since these three powers, or at least the executive and legislative, were interlocked. But so great was Montesquieu's reputation that his view of the English constitution was accepted as correct at the time. The makers of the American constitution utilized his recommendation in separating the three powers of government. (*See Reading No. 14.*)

Tolerance: Milton. The principle of tolerance emerged as one of the most persistent ideas of the Age of Reason. The rationalists argued that even error should be permitted to exist and must not be attacked by reason. It is wrong, they said, to force any man to believe what his reason tells him is false. There is no truth sure enough to justify persecution. This point of view was expressed eloquently by England's greatest epic poet, John Milton (1608-1674). When the Long Parliament in 1643 issued an order regulating the printing, circulation, and importation of books, Milton published his *Areopagitica,* a classic defense of freedom of conscience and speech. Liberty was the central core of Milton's faith, the most powerful, beneficial, and sacred factor in human progress. "It is the liberty, Lords and Commons," he wrote, "which our own valorous and happy counsels have purchased us, liberty, which is the nurse of all great wits. Give me the liberty to know, to utter, and to argue freely according to conscience above all liberties." (*See Reading No. 15.*)

Voltaire and Tolerance. Nothing escaped the fearless, caustic, and irreverent pen of Voltaire, "that mere skeleton with a long nose and eyes of preternatural brilliancy peering out of his wig." In his prodigious literary production he attacked and lampooned royal absolutism, serfdom, slavery, war, ecclesiastical abuses, judicial incompetence, and ignorance. But a recurrent theme was his fierce opposition to intolerance, bigotry, and superstition.

Not only did Voltaire use his powerful pen in the struggle for liberty of conscience, but he also plunged into the battle by opposing intolerance wherever he saw it. So merciless were his attacks that he was forced to spend years in hiding from authorities angered by his philippics. It would be incorrect to regard Voltaire as a crusader for constitutionalism, liberalism, and democracy, but he, nevertheless, helped these causes by his courageous onslaught on intolerance. He popularized the aims and methods of rationalism so successfully that almost the entire literate population of Europe became aware of the ideals of the Age of Reason.

Millions were influenced by what Egon Friedell calls Voltaire's "flaming desire for justice, a burning, consuming, almost drunken hatred for every kind of public despotism, stupidity, malice, or partisanship." The living Voltaire was a leading theorist for benevolent monarchy; by a quirk of fate the dead Voltaire became a powerful propagandist for democracy. Unsuccessful in his attempts to ridicule religion out of existence, he did draw the attention of reasonable men to the necessity for mutual toleration of religious beliefs. Voltaire was said to have written this passage in a letter to Helvétius: "I wholly disapprove of your opinions and will fight to the death for your right to express them!" This may not be authentic, but it does express the fiery nature of a fighter for tolerance. (*See Reading No. 5.*)

Social Contract. The idea of a social contract between people and ruler had been forecast by Plato and had been developed in Roman and medieval thought. Justinian's great code of laws, the *Corpus Iuris Civile,* implied that all rights of legislation resided in the Roman people, but that, by the *Lex Regia,* these rights were transferred to the Emperor. With the revival of Roman law in the Middle Ages, the concept of a social contract was taken over by the temporal authorities as a weapon against the supremacy of the Church. In its general sense, the theory held that authority, resting originally with the people, was conferred by them on the ruler, so that he could perform the necessary functions of state. In the Age of Reason the idea of a social contract was revived as a doctrinal counterbalance to the theory of the divine right of kings. It could be used as a weapon by subjects to justify their resistance to the acts of an unrestrained despot.

There were two possible interpretations of the social contract—the theory could be used to assert the authority of the ruler, or it could be used to show the sovereignty

of the people as the ultimate source of authority. Ernst
Cassirer points out that, in the development of natural
rights the distinction between social contract and contract of sovereignty plays a decisive rôle. "By social
contract [*pactum societis, contrat social*] is understood
that act by which individuals originally united and by
virtue of which they have transcended the mere 'state
of nature.' By virtue of this pact the individuals, the
singuli, are transformed into a real *universitas:* thus
originates the common will, which being established by
free consent (*consensus*) of the individuals has also the
power of obligating them to carry out certain actions.
The contract of subjection (*pactum subjectionis*) was
distinguished from this social contract; it was the pact
by which the community transfers to a sovereign certain
rights originally derived from the social contract."

Hobbes' Version.   In his *Leviathan, or the Matter,
Form, and Power of a Commonwealth, Ecclesiastical
and Civil* (1651), Thomas Hobbes conceived of the
commonwealth or state ("Leviathan") as an artificial
man. "Nature," Hobbes wrote, "the art whereby God
hath made and governs the world, is by the art of man
so imitated that he can make an artificial animal. For
by art is created that great Leviathan called a Commonwealth, or state, which is but an artificial man; in
which the sovereignty is an artificial soul, as giving
life and motion; the magistrates and other officers the
joints; reward and punishment the nerves; concord,
health; discord, sickness; lastly, the pacts or covenants
by which the parts were first set together resembles the
'fiat' of God at the Creation." Hobbes found the origin
of sovereignty in an original compact, whereby man,
weary of war—"the state of nature," agrees to submit
to the authority of an individual or a group strong enough
to maintain order and security. Otherwise, the life of
man must remain "solitary, poor, nasty, brutish, and
short." The common power thus set up at the same time
restrains and protects every individual. The sovereignty
may be in one man, or in a limited assembly, or in
an assembly of all—monarchy, aristocracy, democracy;
these three forms only, though when they are not liked
they are called other names. In any case, the power of

the sovereign is absolute, whether a monarchy or an assembly. It matters not who the sovereign power is, only that he be powerful.

Hobbes himself favored absolute monarchy, which he regarded as a political necessity ("If two men ride upon a horse one must ride in front"), but he was dissatisfied with divine right as a basis for it. Repelled by the Great Rebellion of 1649, Hobbes refused to sanction the right of revolution which the social contract implied. (*See Reading No. 7.*)

Locke's Version. A different version of the social contract was projected by John Locke in his *Two Treatises of Government* (1690), written to justify the Glorious Revolution of 1688. Locke gave these stages in the formation of the social contract:

1. Men originally lived in a state of nature, without law, order, or government, but possessing certain natural rights, such as life, liberty, and property, all of them inalienable, sacred, and inherent in nature.

2. This condition was inconvenient, dangerous, and unsatisfactory, because the strong oppressed the weak, and the life of man was poor and short.

3. The more rational members of society therefore agreed to institute a government to maintain order and to guarantee the enjoyment of man's natural rights. By common consent, an agreement, or social contract, was entered into between rulers and ruled.

4. The contract, or constitution, defined the rights and powers of both rulers and ruled. The people—the ruled—gave up some of their rights to the government but did not surrender their basic, natural rights.

5. The dissolution of the contract—revolution—is justifiable when the terms of the contract are violated by the rulers.

6. Thus, the people are the real rulers, and if a majority of them declare that the contract has been broken, they have the right to rebel and install a new government. Popular sovereignty, it follows, is a precious possession of the people.

Locke's concept of natural rights developed into the most widespread moral philosophy of the Age of Reason. The most characteristic of these rights, though not the fundamental one, was the right to property, grounded on the "self-evident principle" that any person was entitled to any object with which he had mixed the labor of his body.

Popular Sovereignty: Rousseau. The doctrine of the social contract took a revolutionary shape in the hands of Rousseau. His *Le contrat social* (1762) sought to place all government on the consent, direct or implied, of the governed. "Man is born free, and yet is everywhere in chains." Abandoning his originally free state, man had accepted the chains of government. All civil governments exist by virtue of the social contract or agreement, whereby each individual surrenders his rights to the central authority in accordance with the will of all members of the community. If a ruler rejects the sovereignty of the people, and therefore violates the agreement, he must recognize the fact that the people have a natural right to overthrow him. "The essence of the pact," Rousseau wrote, "is the total and unreserved alienation by each partner of all his rights to the community as a whole. No individual can retain any rights that are not possessed equally by all other individuals without the contract thereby being violated. Each partner, in yielding his rights to the community, yields them to no individual, and thus in his relations with individuals he regains all the rights which he has sacrificed. Therefore, the compact may be reduced to the following terms: *'Each of us places in common his person and all his power under the supreme direction of the general will, and we receive each member as an indivisible part of the whole.'* "

The sovereign will, said Rousseau, is the general will. Each individual finds himself in a double relationship. To the general will each partner, by the terms of the contract, must submit himself, without any consideration for his private inclinations. If he refuses to submit, the sovereign will must compel him to do so. In other words, he will be forced to be free. This is necessary, for in the supremacy of the general will lies the only guarantee to each citizen of freedom for personal dependence.

By the very means of passing through the compact from the state of nature to the civil state, man substitutes justice for instinct in his conduct, and gives to his actions a morality of which they were formerly devoid. Man loses by the contract his natural liberty, as well as an illimitable right to all that tempts him and that he can obtain. But what he gains is civil liberty, a precious gain, and the right of secure property in all that he possesses. The social contract, in place of destroying natural liberty, substitutes a moral and legitimate equality for the natural and physical inequality between men. While men may be unequal in strength and talent, they are all equal by convention and right.

Democracy by Natural Right. Rousseau thus converted Locke's projection into a magnificent piece of popular political propaganda. There were fantastic arguments and gaping flaws in Rousseau's exposition of the social contract. Yet, curiously, its mixture of eloquence and logic was exactly the sort of approach that could set the minds of men on fire and carry the multitude with it. Rousseau's *Le contrat social* became one of the most important inspirations for the tremendous events of the French Revolution. The watchwords, "Liberty, Equality, and Fraternity," were taken directly from Rousseau's book. What Rousseau did was to place democracy squarely on the basis of natural rights, systematize it as a conception, and give it direction. In essence, he wanted man to admire the primitive way of life, which he felt to be a happy one; civilization, he said, with its knowledge, laws, and cosmopolitan institutions, had brought only wickedness and misery. Democracy was a natural right of man and it was best suited to his spiritual nature. (*See Readings Nos. 16 and 17.*)

Utilitarianism: Bentham. To the utilitarians it was unimportant whether any scheme of society was natural or divine. What counted was whether it was reasonable and socially useful. To Claude Helvétius man was perfectible if his environment were rationally controlled. This point of view was expressed also by Jeremy Bentham (1748-1832), an English philosopher and jurist, in his *Introduction to Principles of Morals and Legislation* (1789). Bentham defined utility as that property in any object whereby it tends to produce pleasure, good, or happiness, or to prevent the happenings of mischief, evil, or unhappiness to the party whose interest is considered. The principle of utility, he wrote, makes utility the criterion for approval or disapproval of every kind of action. An act which conforms to this principle is one which ought to be done, is right, or, at least, not wrong. There is no other criterion possible which cannot ultimately be reduced to the personal sentiment of the individual.

Bentham believed it to be the business of government to promote the happiness of society by rewarding and punishing, especially by punishing acts tending to diminish happiness. The happiness of the individuals of which a community is composed is the sole end which the legislator ought to have in view. It is also the sole standard, in conformity to which each individual ought to be made to fashion his behavior. The object of all legislation, Bentham wrote, must be the greatest happiness of the greatest number. Happiness can be measured quantitatively. Government should secure as great a degree of individual freedom as possible, since freedom makes for happiness. Those laws that serve the needs of man should be retained, while those that do not should be promptly discarded. Since political, social, and religious freedoms are useful, they should be strongly supported. Since absolutism and mercantilism are not useful, they should be discarded.

The idea of utilitarianism was not new, but Bentham cemented the alliance between utility and happiness, elevated it to the plane of science, and made it into a faith. He placed economics and politics in the serene, impersonal sphere of mathematics. Applied to the discipline of economics, utilitarianism called for free trade, low taxes, efficient government, abolition of monopoly, and unlimited competition. Applied to politics, it called for a constitutional government enforcing security and justice, individual liberty, and civil liberties. All these were useful and hence desirable. These views were supported by James Mill (1773-1836) and his son, John Stuart Mill (1806-1873), both of whom were strongly influenced by Bentham's concept of utilitarianism.

6

THE RISE OF MODERN EXPERIMENTAL SCIENCES

The Experimental Method. The glory of the Age of Reason meant more than the sphere of speculative thinking and theory. The success of seventeenth-century scholars in "mathematicizing the universe" led to the extension of natural law to all the experimental sciences. Fully convinced that they were working in a mechanistic universe controlled by natural law, scientists turned from theology to experimentation and observation to improve their disciplines. Using the telescope, microscope, pendulum clock, barometer, thermometer, and a host of other devices, they set about the task of accumulating a vast amount of accurate data. Discoveries of scientific facts multiplied, and interest in science grew rapidly. New scientific organizations, including the Royal Society of London and the French Academy of Sciences, were founded to encourage scholars, publish scientific treatises, perfect and standardize instruments, and coördinate information. The work of the new scientists had a profound influence on Western civilization, taking rank in importance with the discovery of the New World and the Commercial Revolution.

Medieval Medicine. Medieval medicine was deplorably primitive. There was no anesthesia, nor was there any understanding of sanitation or proper diet. Minor and major surgery was performed by ignorant barbers, whose most important cure-all was blood-letting. Unscrupulous apothecaries mixed fantastic nostrums in the belief that anything stirring up a commotion was bound to do some good. At least one-fourth the population perished when the dreaded Black Death struck Europe in the fourteenth century. At medieval medical schools the final authority on all questions of health and disease was Hippocrates (born 460 B.C.), the Greek

father of medicine. According to Hippocrates, health
and disease resulted from the proper or improper combination of the fluids or humors of the body—blood,
phlegm, black bile, and yellow bile.

The New Medicine. The beginnings of modern
scientific medicine may be traced to three great scientists, Paracelsus, Vesalius, and Paré. Philippus Aureolus
Theophrastus Bombastus von Hohenheim, later called
Paracelsus (c. 1493-1541), a Swiss physician, lectured
at the University of Basel, where he solemnly burned
the works of Hippocrates, Galen, and Avicenna. Dis-
carding the antiquated practice of his profession, he
called for the direct observation of nature as the basis
of medicine. Originator of the doctrine that the life
processes are chemical, he turned to chemistry to seek
remedies for disease. Quarrelsome and impetuous (the
word "bombastic" is derived from one of his middle
names), he was always involved in personal feuds, and
was eventually killed by hirelings of jealous physicians
and apothecaries. Although still handicapped by old
superstitions, Paracelsus was responsible for inaugurating
a new era in internal medicine.

The founder of the modern science of anatomy,
perhaps the most commanding figure in medicine between
Galen and Harvey, was Andreas Vesalius (1514-1564),
a Flemish anatomist and court physician to Charles V.
Vesalius taught anatomy at Padua and other Italian
cities by direct observation of the human body through
dissection. The authorities took a dim view of his activi-
ties. Accused of having opened the body of a Spanish
nobleman before life was extinct, he was forced to
undertake a penitential journey to the Holy Land. His
book, *On the Fabric of the Human Body* (1543), is a
landmark in the history of medicine.

Medieval surgery had been a gory business complicated
by pain, infection, and bleeding. Not until the nineteenth
century was it found possible to ease pain and combat
infection by the use of anesthesia and asepsis, but the
problem of bleeding was successfully met by Ambroise
Paré (c. 1510-1590). Attached to the French army,
Paré treated gunshot wounds, extracted bullets, and
amputated limbs. Previously, battlefield wounds had

been cauterized with boiling oil, but Paré substituted the ligature of arteries for this primitive treatment.

Modern Physiology. In 1628, William Harvey (1578-1657), an English physician, discovered the circulation of blood. Until this time physicians believed that the arteries, as the name suggests, served as air tubes. Making his experiments on the hearts of men, birds, frogs, and fishes, Harvey discovered that blood is pumped from the heart through the arteries, that it returned to the heart through the veins, and that it moves in circular motion through the body. This revolutionary discovery, quickly recognized by the medical world, was an important step in understanding how the human body functions and a vital aid in the control of hemorrhage during operations.

The diagnostic technique of studying blood pressure was discovered by Stephen Hales (1679-1761), an English physiologist, chemist, and inventor. His method was somewhat crude, consisting of attaching a tube to a blood vessel of a horse and measuring the rise of blood in the tube. The principle, however, is much the same as that used by physicians today.

Empirical Medicine. Hermann Boerhaave (1688-1738), a Dutch professor of medicine, founded the science of empirical medicine (emphasizing clinical observation). He made the medical school at Leyden the best institution of its kind in Europe. An expert clinician, he was the first to prove that smallpox is contagious. The beginnings of modern physical diagnosis may be traced to Leopold Auenbrugger (1722-1809), a Viennese physician. Interested in music, he applied his knowledge of acoustics to medicine and discovered the technique of percussion of the thorax (tapping the chest with the fingers). Another important diagnostic device was the stethoscope, invented by René Laënnac (1781-1826), a French physician. Observing one day how children played a game of transmitting sound from one end of a wooden plank to another by scratching a pin, Laënnac devised a simple wooden stethoscope to hear sounds within the chest wall. By thus concentrating the sense of hearing the physician could now detect abnormalities of the heart and chest.

The progress of medicine was assisted by the first of the microbe hunters, Anthony van Leeuwenhoek (1632-1723), a Dutch city-hall janitor. Leeuwenhoek discovered a large number of microscopic bodies, and described them in painstaking reports to the Royal Society of London.

Modern Chemistry. In its early form, alchemy, chemistry was occupied mainly with the art of making silver and gold from the baser metals and the mixing of potions designed to bring eternal youth. A new era began with Robert Boyle (1627-1691), an English natural philosopher, who successfully applied the methods of inductive science to chemistry. The first to distinguish between mixtures and compounds, Boyle showed conclusively that a compound might have different qualities from those of its constituent elements. Boyle's Law (1662) states that the volume of a given mass of gas is inversely proportional to its pressure.

Modern chemistry was deeply concerned with the phenomenon of combustion. Georg Ernst Stahl (1660-1734), a German physician and chemist, projected the doctrine of phlogiston, to the effect that in all things that burn there is an invisible subtle fluid that was not fire itself but the material of fire. This fluid, combining with a calx or ash in combustible bodies, is given off from them when burning takes place. Widely accepted at first, the theory of phlogiston was later disproved.

Hydrogen gas, "inflammable air," was discovered in 1766 by Henry Cavendish (1731-1810), a timid, misanthropic Englishman, whose most important aim in life seemed to have been the necessity of avoiding the attention of his fellow men. In 1784 Cavendish announced his discovery that water resulted from the union of two gases. In the meantime, Joseph Priestly (1733-1804), an English Nonconformist minister and chemist, made his epoch-making discovery of oxygen. Heating red oxide of mercury with a burning-glass, he found that in it a candle burned with a strikingly vigorous flame and that mice lived longer in it than in an equal volume of ordinary air. He concluded that this was not air, but a substance of much greater perfection, which he named dephlogisticated air. Without formal scientific education,

Priestly made other vital discoveries, including the isolation of ammonia, the production of carbon monoxide, and the application of carbon dioxide in aerating waters.

The great trio, Boyle, Cavendish, and Priestly, made many remarkable contributions to chemistry, but all three held the inaccurate idea that phlogiston is removed during the process of combustion. It remained for a French chemist, Antoine Laurent Lavoisier (1743-1794), to destroy the phlogiston legend and give a true explanation of the phenomenon of burning. The first to apply accurate weighing to chemical experimentation, Lavoisier found that no matter how he might do it, the quantity of matter involved in any experiment always remained precisely the same at the end as at the beginning. By heating mercury in a vessel of air, he proved that it gained weight to precisely the extent that the air lost weight. From this Lavoisier reasoned that combustion is a process by which Priestly's dephlogisticated air was taken from ordinary air and united with the substance consumed. He gave the name oxygen to Priestly's discovery. A by-product of Lavoisier's famous experiments was the equally important law of the conservation of matter: *Matter can neither be created nor destroyed, whatever other changes it may undergo.* The entire superstructure of modern chemistry rests upon this basic scientific law. A perverse fate led Lavoisier to the guillotine during the French Revolution.

Physics: From Galileo to Volta. Physics, too, was strongly influenced by the experimental method. Galileo and Newton, who had reduced the study of nature to a few fundamental laws, fashioned the framework upon which others built new scientific laws. Evangelista Torricelli (1608-1647), an Italian physicist, discovered the principle upon which the barometer is based, devised the fundamental principles of hydro-mechanics, and made important improvements on both the telescope and the microscope. Blaise Pascal (1623-1662), a French mathematician, completed Torricelli's experiments by determining conclusively the weight of air and by applying barometric readings to the measurement of heights. Otto von Guericke (1602-1686), a German physicist, invented the air pump and advanced the study of atmospheric pressure. Great strides were made by these scientists in the study of sound, light, heat, elasticity, and electricity.

The modern science of electricity was founded by William Gilbert (1540-1603), an English physician, who, in 1600, laid down theories of terrestrial magnetism and first used the terms electric force and magnetic pole. Benjamin Franklin (1706-1790), the first great American scientist, proved the identity of lightning and electricity in a famous kite experiment in 1752. His invention of the lightning-rod gave him top rank among his contemporary scientists. Luigi Galvani (1737-1798), an Italian physiologist and anatomist, discovered by accident what is called galvanic activity, after observing the convulsive twitching produced in the leg of a skinned frog after contact with the point of a scalpel charged with electricity. Alexander Volta (1745-1827), another Italian university professor, contrived an apparatus for generating electricity that flowed continuously, instead of discharging itself in one spark, as in the old Leyden jar. For this feat Volta was immortalized in the name given to the practical electric unit of electromotive force, the volt (electromotive force applied to a conductor whose resistance is one ohm that will produce a current of one ampere).

Other Sciences. Comparable advances were made in biology, the science of living things, in its two branches —botany, dealing with plants, and zoology, concerned with animals. The new approach, stressing observation and experimentation, brought to light an enormous body of new information on plant and animal life. Carolus Linnaeus (1707-1778), a Swedish naturalist, founded modern botany by working out a celebrated system of plant classification based on differences in sexual characteristics. Before his time plants had been classed as either trees, herbs, or shrubs; Linnaeus proposed new orders, genera, and species, a system still used by botanists.

A similar service was performed for zoology by Comte de Buffon (1707-1788), a French naturalist and superintendent of the Royal Botanical and Zoological Gardens at Paris. Buffon's famous 44-volume *Histoire naturelle* enjoyed great popularity. The public, enthused by the work of both Linnaeus and Buffon, responded zealously by collecting plant and animal specimens.

The science of geology was stimulated by the work of James Hutton (1726-1797), a Scotsman. According to the old catastrophic theory in geology, at a number of successive epochs great revolutions took place on the earth's surface, and all living things were destroyed; after an interval, the world was re-stocked with fresh plants and animals, that, in turn, were destroyed and entombed in the strata of the next revolution. In his *Theory of the Earth* (1785), Hutton rejected the old theory of catastrophe in favor of uniformitarianism, holding that geological processes are always the same and that the geological present should always be explained by the geological past.

The extension of geographical knowledge was made necessary by the new global explorations. Gerardus Mercator (1512-1594), a Flemish mathematician and geographer, invented a new kind of projection, named after him, for drawing of marine charts. Bernhardus Varenius (1622-1650), a German geographer, founded the disciplines of absolute, relative, and comparative geography. His *Geographia Generalis* (1650), a comprehensive treatment of descriptive geography, was concerned with the mathematical and astronomical foundations of geographical science.

7

LITERATURE IN THE ENLIGHTENMENT

Age of Prose. The period from the late seventeenth century to the end of the eighteenth, roughly paralleling the Age of Reason, is also called the Age of Prose. With a diminishing ecclesiastical authority, the emergence of national states, and the growth of popular interest in science, the Western vernacular languages were gradually freed from Latin influence and became standardized. The invention and the rapid development of printing from movable type rendered a more comprehensible literary style necessary. Poetry, the traditional medium of medieval vernacular literature, gave way to prose, considered to be more suitable for a secularized era.

Prelude to Classicism. For several generations after the death of Shakespeare in 1616, English literature reflected the shifting bases of religious strife. John Milton (1608-1674) epitomized the spirit of Puritanism, but at the same time was the precursor of the rationalistic and free-thinking writers of the Age of Reason. Restoration literature presented a strong reaction against the severe Calvinist code. The new approach was apparent in the work of William Wycherley (1640-1716) and William Congreve (1670-1729), whose comedies perfectly mirrored an age of cuckoldry—"the Utopia of gallantry, where pleasure is duty, and the manners perfect freedom." The oncoming spirit of classicism was expressed by John Dryden (1631-1700), man of letters, poet laureate, playwright, and all-round literary genius. From Dryden's prolific pen there flowed biting satires, majestic verse in elaborate baroque structure, rhymed heroic drama, blank verse, and pungent criticism, in short, every conceivable form of literature. Dryden took the English language, which had been polished by Milton and others into cold marble, and endowed it with grace and suppleness. The modern practical prose style stems from this gifted Englishman.

English Classicism. Dryden died in 1700 mourned by the younger generation as a revered master and as the father of English criticism. Momentous changes in society, in literature, and in the arts were taking place. The new age, dominated by the great discoveries of Descartes and Newton, turned to mathematics, reason, nature, and science. Since nature was governed by the operation of a great world-machine, literary forms, too, were moulded to definitive rules and conventions. English writers looked backward past the Elizabethan Age and the Renaissance to the purely classical antiquity—refined, stable, intellectual, and rational. Life, religion, politics, society, all reflected the rationalistic attitude. Unlike the Renaissance writers, the new classicists cultivated a special style of expression and sometimes paid little attention to content.

Perhaps the best expression of the classical spirit in poetry is to be found in the precise and smooth work of Alexander Pope (1688-1744). Spokesman for a rationalistic generation, Pope voiced the spirit of the new age in a form known as the heroic couplet. In 1733 he published his *Essay on Man,* a great didactic poem, comprising a complete system of ethics "vindicating the ways of God to man." The spirit of the day may be sensed in this extract from Pope's poem:

> Look round our world; behold the chain of love
> Combining all below and all above.
> See plastic Nature working to this end,
> The single atoms each to other tend,
> Attract, attracted to, the next in place
> Formed and impelled its neighbour to embrace.
> See matter next, with various life endued,
> Press to one centre still, the general good.
> Grant that the powerful still the weak control;
> Be man the wit and tyrant of the whole. . . .

The classic form was even more popular in prose than in poetry. The greatest satirist of his day, perhaps the most original satirist of any age, was Jonathan Swift (1667-1745), born in Dublin of English parents. Criticizing the politics of his time, Swift wrote the devastating satire, *Gulliver's Travels,* "to vex the world rather than divert it." The world declined to be vexed, and was hugely diverted. For adults this great work was the fiercest and most savage indictment of human follies— wars, quarrels, and vices—ever written; for children, in abridged form, it became a wonderful adventure tale. Swift took the most fantastic of improbabilities and endowed them with an air of veracity. Few books can compare with this classic in imagination and implacable logic.

In journals of opinion, including the *Tatler* and the *Spectator,* essayists poked fun and ridicule at the morals and ethics of their contemporaries. Chance brought together the somewhat pompous Joseph Addison (1672-1719) and the mercurial Richard Steele (1672-1719), who founded the *Spectator* to record an "abstract and brief chronicle" of the manners of the day.

The Modern Novel. The most successful literary innovation of the eighteenth century was the modern novel, a fictitious prose narrative, involving a plot, and exhibiting the passions and sentiments of believable characters. Story-telling in some form had existed since the days of the Old Testament, and the art had been carried on in medieval romances and allegories. The novel was given its modern form by Daniel Defoe (1659-1731) in his *Robinson Crusoe.* Defoe was a journalist who, in 1719, hit upon the idea of writing a book about the adventures of a Scotsman in five years as a castaway on the island of Juan Fernandez off Chile. Using minute "factual" details, the author easily convinced his readers that his story was a true and accurate account based on actual events. Samuel Richardson (1689-1762), a London printer, wrote the first real English novel, *Pamela, or Virtue Unrewarded,* describing the attempts of a gentleman to seduce his virtuous servant-girl. Virtue was rewarded, for Pamela could be won on no other terms than marriage. This enormously popular plot has been used persistently to the present day.

The English novel came of age with Henry Fielding's masterpiece, *The History of Tom Jones.* Rejecting the conventional morality of Richardson, Fielding drew a broader, more humane picture of everyday life. The life story of Tom Jones is rich in humor and understanding, vigorous in style, and keen in its insight into English life and manners. Other eighteenth-century novelists were Laurence Sterne (1713-1768), an eccentric clergyman, whose *Tristram Shandy* contains some of the most incisive character studies in the English language; Tobias Smollett (1721-1771), a surgeon's mate, who wrote realistic sea stories; and Oliver Goldsmith (1728-1774), whose novel, *The Vicar of Wakefield,* was more widely read than any other eighteenth-century book.

Samuel Johnson. Among England's greatest men-of-letters was the renowned Samuel Johnson (1709-1784). Born in Litchfield, the son of a bookseller, Johnson from his birth was afflicted with a malignant scrofula that permanently disfigured his face and injured both his sight and hearing. While at Oxford, the poverty-stricken young man showed signs of a morbid state of brain and nervous system that was to plague him for the remainder of his life. Although suffering privations and discouragement with sullen fortitude, he rapidly gained fame in the literary world, writing essays, criticism, fiction, poems, and satires in a heavy, neo-classical style burdened by an excessive Latinity. The literary circles of the eighteenth century acknowledged him as their intellectual dictator and heaped praise on his edition of Shakespeare, his critical *Lives of the Poets,* and his *Dictionary of the English Language*.

Dr. Johnson was a violent, arrogant individualist, who was capable of plunging to the depths of melancholia verging on insanity or soaring into euphoria at the drop of an epigram. People who did not know him were annoyed by his peculiar habit of muttering to himself in an inaudible undertone. Restless and fidgety, he never remained still for long, but sat like an animated Buddha with his head inclined over his right shoulder, his tremendous trunk swaying backward and forward, and his hand nervously tapping his knee in a set rhythm. His conversation was punctuated with clucking, hissing, whistling, and humming. He was lazy, discourteous, and insolent. He had, nevertheless, an almost overpowering predilection for learning, which shone through the thick outer coating of eccentricity.

All this and much more were recorded by Dr. Johnson's amanuensis, James Boswell, in perhaps the greatest of all biographies. Living in the great man's shadow, Boswell, with amazing industry, took down his companion's words, noted the details of his life and manners, and preserved his most trivial remarks for posterity.

French Literature. Three playwrights dominated the classical period of French literature in the late seventeenth century. Pierre Corneille (1607-1684) produced a series of solemn tragedies, distinguished by eloquence and passion of scenes and speeches and by the power and music of verse. Jean Baptiste Molière (1622-1673) had an uncanny faculty of depicting the manners and customs of his age in character studies ranging from scholars to hypocrites to bores. Jean Racine (1639-1699) composed tragedies in classical style, using Biblical and Greek subjects. That French became to some extent the fashionable language throughout Europe may be attributed to these three masters of drama.

Eighteenth-century prose, notably the works of Voltaire, Rousseau, Condorcet, and others, was often politically partisan in character, and was designed to arouse discontent with Old Régime. The outbreak of the French Revolution was facilitated by a great mass of literary propaganda calling for a changed world.

German Literature. German literature in the Age of Reason was of little distinction until the latter part of the eighteenth century. Whatever literary impulse survived the devastation of the Thirty Years' War was due to French classical models. The first great figure after Luther was Gotthold Ephraim Lessing (1729-1781), playwright and critic, who vigorously criticized the German propensity to imitate French classical drama and who called for a distinctive German national literature. Lessing's comedy, *Minna von Barnhelm* (1763), marked the birth of German drama. His *Nathan the Wise* (1779), a magnificent plea for tolerance, projected the typically rationalistic idea that noble character belongs to no particular creed.

The works of Schiller and Goethe bridged the gap between German classicism and romanticism. Johann Christoph Friedrich von Schiller (1759-1805) was an artist of great moral earnestness and idealism, who transformed philosophy and history into poetry. In a series of plays, notably *The Robbers* (1781), *Wallenstein* (1799), and *Wilhelm Tell* (1804), he expressed the warmth of his own passion for individual liberty. The latter play, depicting the attempts of the Swiss to escape from Austrian oppression, was an impassioned attack upon tyranny, a vivid picture of a truly popular struggle for freedom.

Johann Wolfgang von Goethe (1749-1832) was the chief ornament of German literature and one of the greatest literary figures in history. An enthusiastic student of Shakespeare, he wrote *Götz von Berlichingen* (1771), a prose drama concerned with medieval chivalry, and, like Lessing's work, designed to free German literature from French influence. His *Sorrows of Werther* (1774), an autobiographical novel in the form of letters, described the life of a love-sick young man who eventually commits suicide. The story of the emotional and sensitive Werther, victim of his Storm-and-Stress environment, was popular throughout Europe, heralding the advent of romanticism as a reaction against classicism.

At the head of Goethe's work was the incomparable *Faust* (1790-1833), upon which he labored for the better part of his life. This great story was based on an old Germanic legend about a scholar who was deeply dissatisfied with his lot in life:

> There, now, I've toiled my way quite through
> Law, medicine, and philosophy;
> And, to my sorrow, also thee,
> Theology, with much ado;
> And here I stand, poor human fool,
> As wise as when I went to school.
> Here like a kennel'd cur I lie!
> Therefore, the magic art I'll try,
> From spirit's might and mouth to draw,
> Mayhap, some key to Nature's law.

To gain knowledge of the supernatural realm, Faust makes a compact with the devil, Mephistopheles; in return for twenty-four years of pleasure and delights, Faust would then give up his soul. On this simple tale Goethe dealt with the deepest problems that could engage the mind of man, especially with the antagonism of moral and sensual principles. The inward struggles of Faust, suggesting those of Hamlet, have an irresistible appeal to all human beings who recognize conflicts with which they themselves are concerned. Critics of the master's work agree that Goethe's contribution is a universal humanism of German origin rather than a German humanism of universal impact.

Classics and Classicism. Steele and Addison collaborated on the production of the *Sir Roger de Coverley Papers* for the *Spectator,* from which modern periodical literature may be dated. The letters of Lord Chesterfield (1694-1773) in England and Madame de Sévigné (1626-1696) in France show the polished manners and social customs of the Enlightenment. The *Diary* of Samuel Pepys (1633-1703) gives a wonderfully impressive record of the author's official and personal interests in Restoration England, his disputes with his wife, his extracurricular amours, and the scandals of London. The most impressive historical work of the age was the monumental *Decline and Fall of the Roman Empire,* by Edward Gibbon (1737-1794). Most of this work was classical in style, secular and rational in spirit. In the words of Preserved Smith: "The literature of the eighteenth century may be regarded, from one point of view, as a vast engine for the diffusion of new ideas. For this end it created new forms and animated them with a new spirit. The chief writers were infected with the virus of science, and were stimulated by the emergence of a large reading public for thought and information."

8

ART AND MUSIC

Secularization of Art: Architecture. The gradual emergence of a bourgeois-dominated social order was accompanied by the appearance of a more individualistic, emotional art form and by the frequent choice of secular themes. Art, like society itself, became more secularized. Influences and ideas in art were exchanged from one part of Europe to another during the seventeenth and eighteenth centuries.

The classical Renaissance forms of architecture were gradually modified by the introduction of a grandiose baroque style characterized by irregular contours to suggest motion and, on occasion, by grotesque effects. This tendency had appeared first in Rome, and was later used in such derivative forms as Romanesque and in such related forms as Byzantine. The new baroque rejected the slender, mystical, imaginative Gothic style and, at the same time, amplified the Renaissance character by adding heavy ornament, grandiose lines, curving elements, and elaboration of detail. Italian architects skilfully decorated their churches in exaggerated and profuse style, producing, nevertheless, a brilliant and joyous effect. Giovanni Lorenzo Bernini (1598-1680) designed palaces, churches, and vast open squares with colonnades and fountains, notably the magnificent court of St. Peter's Cathedral in Rome distinguished by its vast space and curving lines.

From Rome the new baroque style spread to all European countries. In each nation the specific form of baroque was moulded to the national temperament and the available building materials. In Spain, José Churriguera (1650-1725) created an architectural style so broken up and swamped by eccentric decoration that the word churrigueresque is now used to describe this type of elaborate, luxuriant architecture. In France, the baroque

developed along a more practical, formal, although still
heavily decorated style. The best specimen was the im-
posing palace of Louis XIV at Versailles, with its classic
statuary, decorative fountains, huge gardens, and row
upon row of elegant hedges. The interior housed splendid
paintings, rich marble, magnificent brocades and tapes-
tries, spacious naves, and the grand Hall of Mirrors. Most
European princes, both great and small, sought to imitate the splendor of Versailles, even if on a minute scale.
Frederick the Great constructed *San Souci* on the French
model, but gave to it a characteristic Germanic pomp,
vigor, and heaviness.

The energetic baroque of the seventeenth century was
succeeded by the carefree frivolity and daintiness of the
rococo style in the eighteenth century. The name is derived from the French *rocailles,* used to designate the
artificial grottoes and fantastic arrangement of rocks in
the gardens of Versailles. The rococo style accurately
portrayed the decadent elegance and stuffed artificiality
of the French aristocracy during the height of the Old
Régime. This form persisted until the end of the century,
when it was replaced by a severe neo-classical style of
architecture.

Painting. The impetus to painting given by the
great Renaissance artists carried over into the Age of
Reason. El Greco, Murillo, and Velásquez in Spain, and
Rubens, Vermeer, and Rembrandt in the Netherlands,
used the Renaissance techniques of *chiaroscuro* (light
and shade) and perspective. Some painters leaned towards the secularized spirit, exaggeration, and pompos-
ity of baroque architecture, others to the frivolous ultra-
elegant style of rococo. Typical of the French rococo
style was the delicate, almost effeminate painting of Jean
Antoine Watteau (1684-1721), who depicted aristocratic
young men and dainty ladies in silks and ribbons as they
made love in leafy parks. In England, Sir Joshua
Reynolds (1723-1792) and Thomas Gainsborough (1727-
1788) were commissioned by the wealthy gentry to
paint flattering portraits. William Hogarth (1697-1764),
rejecting the luxurious halls of the rich, painted wonderfully dexterous and dramatic scenes of taverns, garrets,
and gutters. Towards the end of the eighteenth century,

along with the development of rationalist criticism, painting took on a more democratic character, reacting against light-hearted artificiality and licentiousness.

Sculpture. The baroque spirit carried over into the field of sculpture, which showed the same impressiveness of heroic mass, the same ignoring not only of structure but also of the laws of equilibrium, and a similar exaggeration of style. The classicism of the Renaissance, expressed in rigid, statue-like poses, gave way to emotionally expressive, fervid, and unrestrained movement. Light, shade, and color were now stressed, rather than form and proportion. The work of Bernini, unexcelled in its dramatic impact, recalled the masterpieces of Michelangelo and Donatello.

Music. During the early part of the seventeenth century, music changed from liturgical to secular, from polyphonic to monophonic. Medieval music had been polyphonic, consisting of several tone-series progressing simultaneously according to the rules of counterpoint, creating the majestic atmosphere desired by the Church. In the less complex monophonic form, a single tune or melody was supported by an accompaniment of chords. The contrapuntal technique of Palestrina was succeeded by a more secularized music sponsored by royal, noble, and merchant patrons.

Opera, the earliest form of secular music, appeared in Florence in the late sixteenth century. The style of opera was based on the assumption that one voice had more dramatic potentialities than the complex polyphony of medieval music. The new form of grand opera was distinguished by orchestral preludes, musical episodes, emphasis on solo song and pure melody, and plots based on mythology, classical history, or contemporary political intrigue. The first great master was Claudio Monteverdi (1567-1643), who gave direction to the new musical form. Italian opera enjoyed tremendous popularity throughout Europe. In the eighteenth century, leadership in operatic composition passed from the Italians to the Germans, notably Christoph Willibald Gluck (1714-1787) and Wolfgang Amadeus Mozart (1756-1791).

Georg Friedrich Handel (1685-1759), a German-born, naturalized British subject, was the first outstanding composer of oratorios—sacred compositions for solo voices, chorus, and orchestra. His best-known and most frequently performed composition, the celebrated *Messiah,* had a Biblical but nonliturgical text, and was presented without action, scenery, or costume. Handel also wrote more than forty operas, based on the Italian style, vigorous in dramatic power and marked by deep emotional feeling.

Handel's contemporary, Johann Sebastian Bach (1685-1750), brought the many forms of musical composition, with the exception of opera, to new heights. The greatest organist of his generation, Bach introduced a new system of fingering that had an important influence in the modern art of piano-playing. His orchestral works, chamber music, and sonatas, baroque in spirit, emphasized movement, expressiveness, and dramatic contrast.

The second half of the eighteenth century, called the age of Haydn and Mozart, witnessed a revolution in the art of music. A new instrumental style, homophonic in character and initially fostered by opera, was now applied to orchestral music. The best known form was the sonata, closely bound with the string quartet, the concerto, the symphony, and the overture. The musical capital of the world shifted now from Rome to Vienna. Franz Joseph Haydn (1732-1809), shining light of the Viennese school, was the first great master of the quartet and the symphony, composing 104 symphonies, of which six are regularly heard today. Protégé of the Esterhazy family, Haydn played an important rôle in developing musical composition, elaborating the sonata form, and perfecting the graceful melodic idiom of the minuet. His work was considerably facilitated by the great progress in instrument making. Antonio Stradivarius (1644-1737), the most famous representative of the Cremonse school of violin-making, brought his craft to a state of perfection.

Wolfgang Amadeus Mozart (1756-1791), an Austrian, was the greatest master of the symphony before Beethoven. At the age of six, Wolfgang set out on a European tour, playing the violin, piano, and organ, and creating a profound sensation everywhere. In his brief, poverty-stricken life, Mozart composed some six hundred works, many set apart by a hitherto unapproached richness and variety of expression. Few composers in the history of music have matched his genius in melodic fluency and in mastery of musical forms.

— 9 —

MODERN MAN AND THE AGE OF REASON

Era of Transition. While the main ideas of the Age of Reason were developed in the seventeenth and eighteenth centuries, they were strongly rooted in the past. In this sense the Enlightenment was a typically historical movement, the product of consistent and continuous development. In the fifteenth and sixteenth centuries the medieval spirit clashed head-on with the Renaissance mind, the impact leaving a residue of unresolved problems to which the rationalists turned the strength of their intellect. The men of the Age of Reason did not raise these problems one by one. Their great contribution was to recognize the various questions as elements in a complex whole and to arrange them around a single center—the order of nature. From this point on the rationalists sought to find the laws of nature and to establish a universal moral order. Their search gave form and content to Western thought, despite adjustments and amendments made by nineteenth- and twentieth-century thinkers.

In his *Heavenly City of the Eighteenth-Century Philosophers,* Carl Becker contrasts three separate climates of opinion, in effect summarizing the meaning of the Age of Reason:

Thirteenth Century: In this climate of opinion it was an unquestioned fact that the world and man in it had been created in six days by God, the omniscient and benevolent intelligence, for an ultimate and inscrutable purpose. For the thirteenth-century mind, existence was a cosmic drama, composed by the master dramatist on a central theme and a master plan. The function of intelligence was to demonstrate the truth of revealed knowledge. Philosophy was the science that reconciled nature and history.

Eighteenth Century: In this intellectual era the universe was discovered to be a mechanical machine designed by an efficient engineer or Prime Mover according to the rules of Newtonian physics. The thinkers of the Enlightenment rejected the three stately entrance ways of the Middle Ages—theology, philosophy, and deductive logic —in favor of history, science, and inductive reasoning. The *philosophes* renounced the superstitions and hocus-pocus of medieval thought, but still betrayed their debt to the medieval mind without being aware of it.

Twentieth Century: In our current climate of opinion the vision of man and his world as a neat and efficient machine, designed by an intelligent Author of the Universe, has gradually faded away. Scientists cease to speak with any assurance of the laws of nature. Existence is regarded as "a blindly running flux of disintegrating energy." The trend of modern thought is away from rationalization of the facts to a more careful and disinterested examination of the facts themselves. Facts are primary, stubborn, irreducible. The contemporary thinker rejects both medieval philosophy and eighteenth-century natural philosophy in favor of natural science. New discoveries and inventions are no longer considered to be fortunate accidents that we are expected to note with awe and wonder. "They are all part of the day's work, anticipated, deliberately intended, and brought to pass according to schedule. . . . There is nothing new in heaven or earth not dreamt of in our laboratories."

The Age of Reason, in Becker's analysis, stands midway between the Middle Ages and the modern era, but it is historically related to both. Its underlying conceptions were to some extent the same as those of the thirteenth century, yet it pointed the way to the future. Like all historical movements, it was essentially an age of transition, in which man utilized his knowledge of the past as he looked to the future.

Rationalist Decalogue. What were the attributes of the modern mind and temper that can be traced to that magnificent drama of the human spirit that we call the Age of Reason? We may summarize its basic characteristics in these ten salient points:

1. *Rationalism:* Reason—written by the rationalists with a capital "R"—was enthroned on the seat once held by tradition and authority. The *philosophes* were certain that reason would clear up the fog engendered by faith, revelation, and superstition. It would teach men to control their environments and themselves. "Human reason is not infallible," wrote Lord Chesterfield to his son, "but it will prove to be the least erring guide to follow." Suspend the restraints of reason, warned the rationalists, and beyond them will be found only the primordial violence into which men, when their laws are broken down, will relapse.

2. *Cosmology:* The new rationalist world-view set up a cosmology radically different from that projected by the Greeks or by St. Augustine and St. Thomas Aquinas. It was a new concept of man, his existence on earth, and the place of the earth in the universe. Newton's universal law of nature, subsequently elaborated and tested mathematically, gave a new direction to man in the march of civilization.

3. *Scientific Method:* There was established during the Age of Reason a new scientific method with emphasis upon mathematical analysis, experimentation, and observation. Men perplexed by the mysteries of the universe and the complexities of human behavior were convinced now that they had found the golden key to knowledge. They fashioned a new age of faith in science.

4. *Secularism:* The application of the methods of science to religion and philosophy and the secularization of politics, morals, and ethics are now widely considered to be no less subject to fixed formula than astronomy and physics. The rationalists held all institutions to be amenable to natural law, and urged that all such insti-

tutions be investigated, criticized, and explained in terms
of the new pattern. Both religion and rationalism were
systems of moral values, dedicated to answering the vital
questions; both had essentially the same ethical goals;
both had similar conceptions of evil. But the final spirit
of the Enlightenment was clearly hostile to organized
religion.

5. *Conquest of Superstition:* The faith of the Age of
Reason admitted no supernatural above the natural.
After centuries of conflict, natural reason triumphed
over superstition and the irrational. Modern man rejected the philosopher's stone and the elixir of life and
turned to mathematical formulae and the test-tube.
Rationalism brought man back to his natural habitat—
the earth.

6. *Confidence:* The rationalists were enthusiastically
confident of their power of human understanding. They
were convinced that man is intrinsically good and that
he is able to achieve happiness. Their doctrine of social
progress was unquestionably new and basic in modern
times. They may have exaggerated its import, but at
least they freed the human mind from nearly two
thousand years of restraint and authority. Progress, they
said, was due to the spread of reason, to increasing enlightenment (*les lumières*).

7. *Tolerance:* The eighteenth century witnessed great
strides in the struggle against intolerance and its hamper-
ing effects. The tolerance preached zealously by the
rationalists was a mighty step forward in the moral
pilgrimage of man. Whatever weaknesses the rationalists
may have exhibited, they should be praised for their
attempts to rid the world of the blight of ignorance,
vice, and folly.

8. *Freedom:* The modern battle against despotism
and for freedom of thought and expression began in the
program of the rationalists. Emancipated themselves,
they dedicated themselves to the enterprise of bringing
liberty to all men. They drove home the important point
that man gains freedom in so far as he is able to understand, and through understanding control, the forces of
nature, outside him and inside also.

9. *Legal Reform:* It was to the further glory of the

rationalists that they sought reform of laws in the direction of justice, kindness, and charity, as well as relaxation of persecution of debtors and the delinquent. Montesquieu's *The Spirit of the Laws,* a great sociological treatise, marked a turning point in the history of legal institutions.

10. *Mass Education:* The Age of Reason was responsible for the beginnings of mass education. If it had contributed nothing else, this achievement would have made it one of the truly creative movements of history.

Reaction Against Reason: Romanticism. The conservative mind inevitably reacted against "the self-evident dictates of pure reason." To some extent this reaction was a protest against the excesses of the French Revolution. The nineteenth-century movement, known as romanticism, emphasized the emotional rather than the rational side of human nature, and exalted faith and intuition instead of the intellect. The romantics saw their organic-genetic conception of culture as an expression of the national soul. They issued a plea for the claims of the imagination, of emotion and feeling, of individualism, and, above all, for a synthetic expression of the national genius in all its manifold aspects of philosophy, religion, politics, literature, and art. In interpretating life, nature, and history, they turned away from the rationalists' emphasis upon reason.

Traditional and sentimental thinkers developed a fundamental philosophical defense of their position. Romanticism in philosophy turned into a type of metaphysics known as transcendental idealism, expounded by a group of German thinkers, notably Fichte, Schleiermacher, and Hegel. These writers stressed the emotions —ideals, spirit, and faith—with the same confidence that the rationalists had bestowed upon the intellectual faculties.

The emotional outburst took the form of religious self-consciousness, an intensification of faith, a return to traditionalism, and the revival of supernaturalism and mysticism. Intellectual leaders who were appalled by the assault on the fundamental doctrines of Christianity, especially during the French Revolution, when "Reason" reigned, turned back to the impregnable foundation of

faith. In the Germanies this movement was known as
pietism. In England, John Wesley led an evangelical
revival against rationalism.

Romanticism, a revolt against almost everything the
previous era had represented, including politics and
social life, was destined for a comparatively short life.
By the middle of the nineteenth century, with the introduction of new scientific ideas, particularly evolution, it
became engulfed in a new, rising tide of science. Politi·
cally, it merged with the rising force of nationalism—
the most powerful and persistent phenomenon of modern
times.

Part II

SELECTED READINGS
FROM THE GREAT BOOKS
OF THE AGE OF REASON

FRANCIS BACON: *NOVUM ORGANUM*

Francis Bacon, later Lord Verulam (1561-1626), was profoundly dissatisfied with Aristotle and his medieval disciples, the scholastics. In his famous *Novum Organum, or True Suggestions for the Interpretation of Nature* (1620), one of the last great seminal works of our culture to be written in Latin, he attempted a grand systematization of the new natural philosophy. Instead of seeking truth deductively by syllogistic forms (the basis of Aristotelian philosophy), he recommended the use of induction, systematic observation, and experiment. His great opus called for the precise and methodical study, unfettered by Aristotelian bonds, of all the manifestations of nature. It is the business of man, he said, to be the interpreter of nature; to this end he must turn from words to a study of things as a means of discovering nature's laws. A selection of aphorisms from the *Novum Organum* follows.

✓   ✓   ✓

Aphorisms

On the Interpretation of Nature and the Empire of Man

1. Man, as the minister and interpreter of nature, does and understands as much, as his observations on the order of nature, either with regard to things of the mind, permit him, and neither knows nor is capable of more.

2. The unassisted hand and the understanding left to

itself possess but little power. Effects are produced by the means of instruments and helps, which the understanding requires no less than the hand; and as instruments either promote or regulate the motion of the hand, so those that are applied to the mind prompt or protect the understanding.

3. Knowledge and human power are synonymous, since the ignorance of the cause frustrates the effect; for nature is only subdued by submission, and that which in contemplative philosophy corresponds with the cause in practical science becomes the rule.

4. Man whilst operating can only apply or withdraw natural bodies; nature internally performs the rest.

5. Those who become practically versed in nature are, the mechanic, the mathematician, the physician, the alchemist, and the magician, but all (as matters now stand) with faint efforts and meagre success.

6. It would be madness and inconsistency to suppose that things which have never yet been performed can be performed without employing some hitherto untried means.

7. The creations of the mind and hand appear very numerous, if we judge by books and manufactures; but all that variety consists of an excessive refinement, and of deductions from a few well-known matters—not of a number of axioms.

8. Even the effects already discovered are due to chance and experiment, rather than to the sciences; for our present sciences are nothing more than peculiar arrangements of matters already discovered, and not methods for discovery or plans for new operations.

9. The sole cause and root of almost every defect in the sciences is this, that while we falsely admire and extol the powers of the human mind, we do not search for its real helps.

10. The subtlety of nature is far beyond that of sense or of the understanding; so that the specious meditations, speculations, and theories of mankind are but a kind of insanity, only there is no one to stand by and observe it.

11. As the present sciences are useless for the discovery of effects, so the present system of logic is useless for the discovery of the sciences. . . .

18. The present discoveries in science are such as lie immediately beneath the surface of common notions. It is necessary, however, to penetrate the more secret and remote parts of nature, in order to abstract both notions and axioms from things by a more certain and guarded method.

19. There are and can exist but two ways of investigating and discovering truth. The one hurries on rapidly from the senses and particulars to the most general axioms, and from them, as principles and their supposed indisputable truth, derives and discovers the intermediate axioms. This is the way now in use. The other constructs its axioms from the senses and particulars, by ascending continually and gradually, till it finally arrives at the most general axioms, which is the true but unattempted way. . . .

31. It is in vain to expect any great progress in the sciences by superinducing or engrafting new matters upon old. An instauration must be made from the very foundations, if we do not wish to revolve forever in a circle, making only some slight and contemptible progress.

32. The ancient authors and all others are left in undisputed possession of their honors; for we enter into no comparison of capacity or talent, but of method, and assume the part of a guide rather than a critic. . . .

35. Alexander Borgia said of the expedition of the French into Italy that they came with chalk in their hands to mark up their lodgings, and not with weapons to force their passage. Even so do we wish our philosophy to make its way quietly into those minds that are fit for it, and of good capacity; for we have no need of contention where we differ in first principles, and in our very notions, and even in our forms of demonstration.

36. We have but one simple method of delivering our sentiments, namely, we must bring men to particulars and their regular series and order, and they must for a while renounce their notions, and begin to form an acquaintance with things.

37. Our method and that of the sceptics agree in some respects at first setting out, but differ most widely, and are completely opposed to each other in their conclusion;

for they roundly assert that nothing can be known; we, that but a small part of nature can be known, by the present method; their next step, however, is to destroy the authority of the senses and understanding, whilst we invent and supply them with assistance.

38. The idols and false notions which have already preoccupied the human understanding, and are deeply rooted in it, not only so beset men's minds that they become difficult of access, but even where access is obtained will again meet and trouble us in the instauration of the sciences, unless mankind when forewarned guard themselves with all possible care against them.

39. Four species of idols beset the human mind, to which (for distinction's sake) we have assigned names, calling the first Idols of the Tribe, the second Idols of the Den, the third Idols of the Market, the fourth Idols of the Theatre. . . .

41. The idols of the tribe are inherent in human nature and the very tribe or race of man; for man's sense is falsely asserted to be the standard of things; on the contrary, all the perceptions both of the senses and the mind bear reference to man and not to the universe, and the human mind resembles those uneven mirrors which impart their own properties to different objects, from which rays are emitted and distort and disfigure them.

42. The idols of the den are those of each individual; for everybody (in addition to the errors common to the race of man) has his own individual den or cavern, which intercepts and corrupts the light of nature, either from his own peculiar or singular disposition, or from his education and intercourse with others, or from his reading, and the authority acquired by those whom he reverences or admires, or from the different impressions produced on the mind, as it happens to be preoccupied and predisposed, or equable and tranquil, and the like; so that the spirit of man (according to its several dispositions), is variable, confused, and, as it were, actuated by chance; and Heraclitus said well that men search for knowledge in lesser worlds, and not in the greater or common world.

43. There are also idols formed by the reciprocal

intercourse and society of man with man, which we call idols of the market, from the commerce and association of men with each other; for men converse by means of language, but words are formed at the will of the generality, and there arises from a bad and unapt formation of words a wonderful obstruction to the mind. Nor can the definitions and explanations with which learned men are wont to guard and protect themselves in some instances afford a complete remedy—words still manifestly force mankind into vain and innumerable controversies and fallacies.

44. Lastly, there are idols which have crept into men's minds from the various dogmas of peculiar systems of philosophy, and also from the perverted rules of demonstration, and these we denominate idols of the theatre: for we regard all the systems of philosophy hitherto received or imagined, as so many plays brought out and performed, creating fictitious and theatrical worlds. Nor do we speak only of the present systems, or of the philosophy and sects of the ancients, since numerous other plays of a similar nature can still be composed and made to agree with each other, the causes of the most opposite errors being generally the same. Nor, again, do we allude merely to general systems, but also to many elements and axioms of sciences which have become inveterate by tradition, implicit credence, and neglect. . . .

— Reading No. 2 —

DESCARTES: *DISCOURSE ON METHOD*

René Descartes (1596-1650), from whose latinized surname, Cartesius, the title of his philosophy, Cartesianism, is derived, was dissatisfied with the state of learning in his day, and set out on the adventure of finding the right method for obtaining knowledge. The result of this search was a landmark in the modern history of philosophic thought—*Discourse on the Method of Rightly Conducting the Reason and Seeking Truth in the Sciences,* first published in 1637. To Descartes it was clear that reason, the faculty distinguishing truth from error and separating men from brutes, must be the guiding light of human life. The following selection from the *Discourse on Method,* written in the form of an autobiographical treatise, gives the principles of logic that Descartes used with "firm and unwavering resolution."

↗   ↗   ↗

Among the branches of Philosophy, I had, at an earlier period, given some attention to Logic, and among those of the Mathematics to Geometrical Analysis and Algebra,—three Arts or Sciences which ought, as I conceived, to contribute something to my design. But, on examination, I found that, as for Logic, its syllogisms and the majority of its other precepts are of avail rather in the communication of what we already know, or even as the Art of Lully, in speaking without judgment of things of which we are ignorant, than in the investigation of the unknown; and although this Science contains indeed a number of correct and very excellent precepts, there are, nevertheless, so many others, and these either injurious or superfluous, mingled with the former, that it is almost quite as difficult to effect a severance of the true from the false as it is to extract a Diana or a Minerva from a rough block of marble. Then as to the Analysis of the ancients and the Algebra of the moderns, besides that they embrace only matters highly abstract, and, to appearance, of no use, the former is so exclusively restricted to the consideration of figures, that it can exercise the Understanding only on condition of greatly fatiguing the Imagination; and, in the latter, there is so complete a subjection to certain rules and formulas, that there results an art full of confusion and obscurity calculated to embarrass, instead of a science fitted to cultivate the mind. By these considerations I was induced to seek some other Method which would comprise the advantages of the three and be exempt from their defects. And as a multitude of laws often only hampers justice, so that a state is best governed when, with few laws, these are rigidly administered; in like manner, instead of the great number of precepts of which Logic is composed, I believed that the four following would prove perfectly sufficient for me, provided I took the firm and unwavering resolution never in a single instance to fail in observing them.

The FIRST was never to accept anything for true which I did not clearly know to be such; that is to say, carefully to avoid precipitancy and prejudice, and to comprise nothing more in my judgment than what was presented to my mind so clearly and distinctly as to exclude all ground of doubt.

The SECOND, to divide each of the difficulties under examination into as many parts as possible, and as might be necessary for its adequate solution.

The THIRD, to conduct my thoughts in such order that by commencing with objects the simplest and easiest to know, I might ascend by little and little, and, as it were, assigning in thought a certain order even to those objects which in their own nature do not stand in a relation of antecedence and sequence.

At the LAST, in every case to make enumerations so complete, and reviews so general, that I might be assured that nothing was omitted.

The long chains of simple and easy reasonings by means of which geometers are accustomed to reach the conclusions of their most difficult demonstrations, had led me to imagine that all things, to the knowledge of which man is competent, are mutually connected in the same way, and that there is nothing so far removed from us as to be beyond our reach, or so hidden that we cannot discover it, provided only we abstain from accepting the false for the true, and always preserve in our thoughts the order necessary for the deduction of one truth from another. And I had little difficulty in determining the objects with which it was necessary to commence, for I was already persuaded that it must be with the simplest and easiest to know, and considering that of all those who have hitherto sought truth in the Sciences, the mathematicians alone have been able to find any demonstrations, that is, any certain and evident reasons, I did not doubt but that such must have been the rule of their investigations.

I resolved to commence, therefore, with the examination of the simplest objects, not anticipating, however, from this any other advantage than that to be found in accustoming my mind to the love and nourishment of truth, and to a distaste for all such reasonings as were unsound. But I had no intention on that account of attempting to master all the particular Sciences commonly denominated Mathematics: but observing that, however different their objects, they all agree in considering only the various relations or proportions subsisting among those objects, I thought it best for my purpose to consider these proportions in the most general form possible, without referring them to any objects in particular, except such as would most facilitate the knowledge of them, and without by any means restricting them to these, that afterwards I might thus be the better able to apply them to every other class of objects to which they are legitimately applicable. Perceiving further, that in order to understand these relations I should sometimes have to consider them one by one, and sometimes only to bear them in mind, or embrace them in the aggregate, I thought that, in order the better to consider them individually, I should view them as subsisting between straight lines, than which I could find no objects more simple, or capable of being more distinctly represented to my imagination and senses; and on the other hand that in order to retain them in the memory, or embrace an aggregate of many, I should express them by certain characters the briefest possible. In this way I believed that I could borrow all that was best both in Geometrical Analysis and in Algebra, and correct all the defects of the one by help of the other.

And, in point of fact, the accurate observance of these few precepts gave me, I take the liberty of saying, such ease in unraveling all the questions embraced in these two sciences, that in the two or three months I devoted to their examination, not only did I reach solutions of questions I had formerly deemed exceedingly difficult, but even as regards questions of the solution of which I continued ignorant, I was enabled, as it appeared to me, to determine the means whereby, and the extent to which, a solution was possible; results attributable to the circumstance that I commenced with the simplest and most general truths, and that thus each truth discovered was a rule available in the discovery of subsequent ones. Nor in this perhaps shall I appear too vain, if it be considered that, as the truth on any particular point is one, whoever apprehends the truth, knows all that on that point can be known. The child, for example, who has been instructed in the elements of Arithmetic, and has made a particular addition, according to rule, may be assured that he has found, with respect to the sum of the numbers before him, all that in this instance is within the reach of human genius. Now, in conclusion, the Method which teaches adherence to the true order, and an exact enumeration of all the conditions of the thing sought includes all that gives certitude to the rules of Arithmetic.

But the chief ground of my satisfaction with this

Method was the assurance I had of thereby exercising my reason in all matters, if not with absolute perfection, at least with the greatest attainable by me: besides, I was conscious that by its use my mind was becoming gradually habituated to clearer and more distinct conceptions of its objects; and I hoped also, from not having restricted this Method to any particular matter, to apply it to the difficulties of the other Sciences, with not less success than to those of Algebra. I should not, however, on this account have ventured at once on the examination of all the difficulties of the Sciences which presented themselves to me, for this would have been contrary to the order prescribed in the Method, but observing that the knowledge of such is dependent on principles borrowed from Philosophy, in which I found nothing certain, I thought it necessary, first of all to endeavor to establish its principles. And because I observed, besides, that an inquiry of this kind was of all others of the greatest moment, and one in which precipitancy and anticipation in judgment were most to be dreaded, I thought that I ought not to approach it till I had reached a more mature age (being at that time but twenty-three), and had first of all employed much of my time in preparation for the work, as well by eradicating from my mind all the erroneous opinions I had up to that moment accepted, as by amassing variety of experience to afford materials for my reasonings, and by continually exercising myself in my chosen Method with a view to increased skill in its application.

— Reading No. 3 —

NEWTON: *MATHEMATICAL PRINCIPLES OF NATURAL PHILOSOPHY*

Sir Isaac Newton (1642-1727), Lucasian professor of mathematics at Cambridge University when he was only twenty-seven years old, is recognized as the greatest of the seventeenth-century scientific synthesizers. Newton's name, says John Herman Randall, "became a symbol which called up the picture of the scientific machine-universe, the last word in science, one of those uncriticized preconceptions which largely determine the social and political and religious as well as the strictly scientific thinking of the age. Newton *was* science, and science was the eighteenth-century ideal." Newton's *Mathematical Principles of Natural Philosophy,* written in 1687 in Latin, was eventually translated into all the major languages of the world and became the solid foundation of later scientific thought. The following selections, giving definitions, axioms, and rules of reasoning in philosophy, illustrate the qualities of Newton's monumental work of synthesis.

✔ ✔ ✔

Definitions

Definition I

The quantity of matter is the measure of the same, arising from its density and bulk conjointly.

105

Thus air of a double density, in a double space, is quadruple in quantity; in a triple space, sextuple in quantity. The same thing is to be understood of snow, and fine dust or powders, that are condensed by compression or liquefaction, and of all bodies that are by any causes whatever differently condensed. I have no regard in this place to a medium, if any such there is, that freely pervades the interstices between the parts of bodies. It is this quantity that I mean hereafter everywhere under the name of body or mass. And the same is known by the weight of each body, for it is proportional to the weight, as I have found by experiments on pendulums, very accurately made, which shall be shown hereafter.

Definition II

The quantity of motion is the measure of all the same, arising from the velocity and quantity of matter conjointly.

The motion of the whole is the sum of the motion of all the parts; and therefore in a body double in quantity, with equal velocity, the motion is double; with twice the velocity, it is quadruple. . . .

Definition IV

An impressed force is an action exerted upon a body, in order to change its state, either of rest, or of uniform motion in a right line.

This force consists in the action only, and remains no longer in the body when the action is over. For a body maintains every new state it acquires, by its inertia only. But impressed forces are of different origins, as from percussion, from pressure, from centripetal force. . . .

Definition VI

The absolute quantity of a centripetal force is the measure of the same, proportional to the efficacy of the cause that propagates it from the centre, through the spaces round about.

Thus the magnetic force is greater in one loadstone and less in another, according to their sizes and strength of intensity.

Definition VII

The accelerative quantity of a centripetal force is the measure of the same, proportional to the velocity which it generates in a given time.

Thus the force of the same loadstone is greater at a less distance, and less at a greater: also the force of gravity is greater in valleys, less on tops of exceedingly high mountains; and yet less, at greater distances from the body of the earth; but at equal distances, it is the same everywhere; because (taking away, allowing for, the resistance of air), it equally accelerates all falling bodies, whether heavy or light, great or small. . . .

Axioms, or Laws of Motion

Law I

Every body continues in its state of rest, or of uniform motion, in a right line, unless it is compelled to change that state by forces impressed upon it.

Projectiles continue in their motions, so far as they are not retarded by the resistance of the air, or impelled downwards by the force of gravity. A top, whose parts by their cohesion are continually drawn aside from rectilinear motions, does not cease its rotation, otherwise than as it is retarded by the air. The greater bodies of the planets and comets, meeting with less resistance in freer spaces, preserve their motions both progressive and circular for a much longer time.

Law II

The change of motion is proportional to the motive force impressed; and is made in the direction of the right line in which that force is impressed.

If any force generates a motion, a double force will generate double the motion, a triple force triple the motion, whether that force be impressed altogether and at once or gradually and successively. And this motion (being always directed the same way with the generating force), if the body moved before, is added to or subtracted from the former motion, according as they directly conspire with or are directly contrary to each

other; or obliquely joined, when they are oblique, so as
to produce a new motion compounded from the determination of both.

Law III

*To every action there is always opposed an equal reac-
tion: or, the mutual actions of two bodies upon each
other are always equal, and directed to contrary parts.*
Whatever draws or presses another is as much drawn
or pressed by that other. If you press a stone with your
finger, the finger is also pressed by the stone. If a horse
draws a stone tied to a rope, the horse (if I may say so)
will be equally drawn back towards the stone; for the
distended rope, by the same endeavor to relax or unbend
itself, will draw the horse as much towards the stone as
it does the stone towards the horse, and will obstruct the
progress of the one as much as it advances that of the
other. If a body impinge upon another, and by its force
change the motion of the other, that body also (because
of the equality of the mutual pressure) will undergo an
equal change, in its own motion, towards the contrary
part. The changes made by these actions are equal, not
in the velocities but in the motions of the bodies; that
is to say, if the bodies are not hindered by any other
impediments. For, because the motions are equally
changed, the changes of the velocities made toward contrary parts are inversely proportional to the bodies. . . .

Rules of Reasoning in Philosophy

Rule I

*We are to admit no more causes of natural things
than such as are both true and sufficient to explain their
appearances.*
To this purpose the philosophers say that Nature does
nothing in vain, and more is in vain when less will serve;
for Nature is pleased with simplicity, and affects not the
pomp of superfluous causes.

Rule II

*Therefore to the same natural effects we must, as far
as possible, assign the same causes.*

As to respiration in a man and in a beast; the descent of stones in *Europe* and in *America;* the light of our culinary fire and of the sun; the reflection of light in the earth, and in the planets.

Rule III

The qualities of bodies, which admit neither intensification nor remission of degrees, and which are found to belong to all bodies within the reach of our experiments, are to be esteemed the universal qualities of all bodies whatsoever.

For since the qualities of bodies are only known to us by experiments, we are to hold for universal all such as universally agree with experiments; and such as are not liable to diminution can never be quite taken away. We are certainly not to relinquish the evidence of experiments for the sake of dreams and vain fictions of our own devising; nor are we to recede from the analogy of Nature, which is wont to be simple, and always consonant to itself. We no other way know the extension of bodies than by our senses, nor do these reach it in all bodies; but because we perceive extension in all that are sensible, therefore we ascribe it universally to all others also. That abundance of bodies are hard, we learn by experience; and because the hardness of the whole arises from the hardness of the parts, we therefore justly infer the hardness of the undivided particles not only of the bodies we feel but of all others. That all bodies are impenetrable, we gather not from reason but from sensation. The bodies which we handle we find impenetrable, and thence conclude impenetrability to be a universal property of all bodies whatsoever. That all bodies are movable, and endowed with certain power (which we call the inertia) of persevering in their motion, or in their rest, we only infer from the like properties observed in the bodies which we have seen. The extension, hardness, impenetrability, mobility, and inertia of the whole, result from the extension, hardness, impenetrability, mobility, and inertia of the parts; and hence we conclude the least particles of all bodies to be also all extended, and hard and impenetrable, and movable, and endowed with their proper inertia. And this is the foundation of all philosophy. Moreover, that the divided but contiguous particles of bodies may be separated from one another, is matter of observation; and, in the particles that remain undivided, our minds are able to distinguish yet lesser parts, as is mathematically demonstrated. But whether the parts so distinguished, and not yet divided, may, by the powers of Nature, be actually divided and separated from one another, we cannot certainly determine. Yet, had we the proof of but one experiment that any undivided particle, in breaking a hard and solid body, suffered a division, we might by virtue of this rule conclude that the undivided as well as the divided particles may be divided and actually separated to infinity.

Lastly, if it universally appears, by experiments and astronomical observations, that all bodies about the earth gravitate towards the earth, and that in proportion to the quantity of matter which they severally contain; that the moon likewise, according to the quantity of its matter, gravitates towards the earth; that, on the other hand, our sea gravitates towards the moon; and all the planets one towards another; and the comets in like manner towards the sun; we must, in consequence of this rule, universally allow that all bodies whatsoever are endowed with a principle of mutual gravitation. For the arguments from the appearances concludes with more force for the universal gravitation of all bodies than for their impenetrability; of which, among those in the celestial regions, we have no experiments, nor any manner of observation. Not that I affirm gravity to be essential to bodies: by their *vis insita* I mean nothing but their inertia. This is immutable. Their gravity is diminished as they recede from the earth.

Rule IV

In experimental philosophy we are to look upon propositions inferred by general induction from phenomena as accurately or very nearly true, notwithstanding any contrary hypotheses that may be imagined, till such time as other phenomena occur, by which they may either be made more accurate, or liable to exceptions.

This rule we must follow, that the argument of induction may not be evaded by hypotheses.

— Reading No. 4 —

SPINOZA: *ETHICS*

To Baruch Spinoza (1632-1677) God and the universe were one. At the age of twenty-four, the Amsterdam Jew was excommunicated by his synagogue for heretical opinions that God might have a body (that is, the whole world of matter), that angels might be mere visions of the mind, and that the Bible says nothing concerning the immortality of the soul. God, for Spinoza, was simply the universe, in all its extent and with all its details. For this concept of pantheism Spinoza was reviled by many of his contemporaries. But in 1882, at the dedication of the statue of Spinoza at The Hague, Renan delivered this eulogy:

> Woe to him who in passing should hurl an insult at this gentle and pensive head! He would be punished, as all vulgar souls are punished, by his very vulgarity, and by his incapacity to conceive what is divine. This man, from his granite pedestal, will point out to all men the way of blessedness which he found; and in ages hence, the cultivated traveler, passing by this spot, will say in his heart: "The truest vision ever had of God came, perhaps, here."

Several key definitions, axioms, and propositions by which Spinoza sought to prove the existence of God are given here from the *Ethics*.

111

Concerning God

Definitions

I. I understand that to be CAUSE OF ITSELF (*causa sui*) whose essence involves existence and whose nature cannot be conceived unless existing.

II. That thing is said to be FINITE IN ITS KIND (*in suo genere finita*) which can be limited by another thing of the same kind. *E.g.*, a body is said to be finite because we can conceive another larger than it. Thus a thought is limited by another thought. But a body cannot be limited by a thought, nor a thought by a body.

III. I understand SUBSTANCE (*substantia*) to be that which is in itself and is conceived through itself: I mean that, the conception of which does not depend on the conception of another thing from which it must be formed.

IV. An ATTRIBUTE (*attributum*) I understand to be that which the intellect perceives as constituting the essence of a substance.

V. By MODE (*modus*) I understand the modifications (*affectiones*) of a substance or that which is in something else through which it may be conceived.

VI. God (*Deus*) I understand to be a being absolutely infinite, that is, a substance consisting of infinite attributes, each of which expresses eternal and infinite essence.

Explanation.—I say absolutely infinite, but not in its kind. For of whatever is infinite only in its kind, we may deny the attributes to be infinite; but what is absolutely infinite appertains to the essence of whatever expresses essence and involves no denial.

VII. That thing is said to be FREE (*libera*) which exists by the mere necessity of its own nature and is determined in its actions by itself alone. That thing is said to be NECESSARY (*necessaria*) or rather COMPELLED (*coacta*), when it is determined in its existence and actions by something else in a certain fixed ratio.

VIII. I understand ETERNITY (*aeternitas*) to be

existence itself, in so far as it is conceived to follow necessarily from the definition of an eternal thing.

Explanation.—For the existence of a thing, as an eternal truth, is conceived to be the same as its essence, and therefore cannot be explained by duration or time, although duration can be conceived as wanting beginning and end.

Axioms

I. All things which are, are in themselves or in other things.

II. That which cannot be conceived through another thing must be conceived through itself.

III. From a given determined cause an effect follows of necessity, and on the other hand, if no determined cause is granted, it is impossible that an effect should follow.

IV. The knowledge of effect depends on the knowledge of cause, and involves the same.

V. Things which have nothing in common reciprocally cannot be comprehended reciprocally through each other, or, the conception of the one does not involve the conception of the other.

VI. A true idea should agree with its ideal (*ideatum*), *i.e.*, what it conceives.

VIII. The essence of that which can be conceived as not existing does not involve existence.

Propositions

PROP. I.—A substance is prior in its nature to its modification.

Proof.—This is obvious from Definitions III and V. . . .

PROP. IV.—Two or three distinct things are distinguished from the other either by the difference of the attributes of the substances or by the difference of their modifications.

Proof.—All things that are, are either in themselves or in other things (Axiom I), that is (Definitions III and V), beyond the intellect nothing is granted save substances and their modifications. Nothing therefore is granted beyond the intellect, through which several things may be distinguished one from the other except substances, or what is the same thing (Axiom IV), their attributes or modifications. *Q.e.d.*

PROP. V.—In the nature of things, two or more things may not be granted having the same nature or attribute.

Proof.—If several distinct substances are given, they must be distinguished one from the other either by the difference of their attributes or their modifications (previous Proposition). If, then, they are to be distinguished by the difference of their attributes, two or more cannot be granted having the same attribute. But if they are to be distinguished by the difference of their modifications, since a substance is prior in its nature to its modification (Proposition I), therefore let the modifications be laid aside and let the substance itself be considered in itself, that is (Definitions III and VI), truly considered, and it could not then be distinguished from another, that is (previous Proposition), two or more substances cannot have the same nature or attribute. *Q.e.d.* . . .

PROP. VII.—Existence appertains to the nature of substance.

Proof.—A substance cannot be produced from anything else: it will therefore be its own cause, that is (Definition I), its essence necessarily involves existence, or existence appertains to the nature of it. *Q.e.d.* . . .

PROP. XI.—God or a substance consisting of infinite attributes, each of which expresses eternal and infinite essence, necessarily exists.

Proof.—If you deny it, conceive, if it be possible, that God does not exist. Then (Axiom VII) his essence does not involve existence. But this (Proposition VII) is absurd. Therefore God necessarily exists. *Q.e.d.* . . .

PROP. XIV.—Except God no substance can be granted or conceived.

Proof.—As God is a being absolutely infinite, to whom no attribute expressing the essence of substance can be denied (Definition VI), and as he necessarily exists (Proposition XI), if any other substance than God be given, it must be explained by means of some attribute of God, and thus two substances would exist possessing the same attribute, which (Proposition V) is absurd; and so no other substance than God can be granted, and consequently not even be conceived. For if it can be conceived it must necessarily be conceived as existing, and this by the first part of this proof is absurd. Therefore except God no substance can be granted or conceived. *Q.e.d.*

Corollary I.—Hence it distinctly follows that (1) God is one alone, *i.e.*, there is none like him, or in the nature of things only one substance can be granted, and that is absolutely infinite. . . .

Corollary II.—It follows, in the second place, that extension and thought are either attributes of God or modifications of attributes of God.

— Reading No. 5 —

VOLTAIRE: *PHILOSOPHICAL DICTIONARY*

François-Marie Arouet (1694-1778), known by his
assumed name of Voltaire, was born at Paris the son
of a well-to-do notary, and was educated by the Jesuits
in the Collège Louis-le-Grand. He never ceased speculating and satirizing, a tendency that led to his twice
being exiled from Paris and twice imprisoned in the
Bastille. Poet of a royal court, friend of princes and
politicians, idol of beautiful women, gambler and wit,
this long-nosed, beady-eyed rebel lived a full life, dying
when he was eighty-four from exhaustion after a party
in his honor. His life span covered nearly the whole of
the eighteenth century, of which he was the dominant
literary symbol, producing masterpieces in every depart-
ment of letters then in vogue. These extracts from his
Philosophical Dictionary illustrate his biting satire and
his conception of Deism (Theism). Note particularly
his oft quoted essay on tolerance.

✔   ✔   ✔

General Reflection on Man

It needs twenty years to lead man from the plant state
in which he is within his mother's womb, and the pure
animal state which is the lot of his early childhood, to
the state at which the maturity of his reason begins to
appear. It has taken some thirty centuries to learn a
little about his structure. It would need an eternity to

learn something about his soul. It takes but an instant to kill him.

Superstition

The superstitious man is to the rogue what the slave is to the tyrant. Further still, the superstitious man is governed by the fanatic and himself becomes fanatic. Born in paganism, superstition was adopted by Judaism, and infested the Christian Church from the earliest times. All the Fathers of the Church, without any exception, believed in the power of magic. The Church herself always condemned magic, but she nevertheless always believed in it. She did not excommunicate sorcerers as mistaken madmen, but as men who were in reality in communication with the devil.

To-day a half of Europe thinks that the other half has long been and still is under the influence of superstition. The Protestants look upon relics, indulgences, mortifications, prayers for the dead, holy water, and all the rites of the Roman Church, as superstitious dementia. According to them, superstition consists in taking useless practices for necessary practices. Among the Roman Catholics there are some more enlightened than their ancestors, who have renounced many of the usages formerly regarded as sacred; they defend themselves against the others who have retained them by saying: "They are indifferent, and what is merely indifferent cannot be classed as an evil."

It would be difficult to set the limits of superstition. A Frenchman traveling in Italy finds almost everything superstitious, and he is hardly mistaken. The Archbishop of Canterbury insists that the Archbishop of Paris is superstitious; the Presbyterians make the same allegation about His Grace of Canterbury, and they in their turn are treated as superstitious by the Quakers, who are the most superstitious of all in the eyes of other Christians.

In Christian societies, therefore, no one agrees as to what superstition is. The sect which seems to be the least attacked by this malady of the intelligence is that which has the fewest rites. . . .

The less superstition, the less fanaticism; and less fanaticism, the less misery.

Theist

The theist is a man firmly persuaded of the existence of a Supreme Being as good as He is powerful, who has formed all beings with extension, vegetating, sentient and reflecting, who perpetuates their species, who punishes crime without cruelty, and rewards virtuous actions with kindness.

The theist does not know how God punishes, how He protects, how He pardons, for he is not reckless enough to flatter himself that he knows how God acts, but he does know that God acts and that He is just. Difficulties against Providence do not shake him in his faith, because they remain merely great difficulties, and not proofs. He submits to this Providence, even though he perceives but a few effects and a few signs of this Providence, and, judging the things he does not see by the things which he does see, he considers that this Providence reaches all places and all centuries.

Reconciled with the rest of the universe by this principle, he does not embrace any of the sects, all of which contradict one another. His religion is really the oldest and most widespread, for the simple worship of God has come before all the systems of the world. He speaks a language that all peoples understand, while they do not understand one another. He has his brothers from Peking to Cayenne, and he numbers all wise men among his brethren. He believes that religion does not consist either in the opinions of an unintelligible metaphysics, or in vain display, but in worship and justice. He finds his service in doing good. His doctrine is being submissive to God. The Muslim cries to him: "Be careful if you do not make the pilgrimage to Mecca!" "Woe unto you," says a Recollet, "if you do not make a pilgrimage to Notre Dame de Lorette!" He laughs at Lorette and at Mecca. But he succors the needy and defends the oppressed.

Tolerance

What is tolerance? It is the consequence of humanity. All of us are formed of frailty and error. Let us mutually pardon each other's folly. That is the first law of nature.

It is quite clear that the individual who persecutes a man, his brother, because he is not of the same opinion, is nothing more than a monster. That admits of no difficulty. But the Government! The Magistrates! The Princes! How do they treat those who have different worships from theirs? If they are powerful strangers, it is certain that a prince will make an alliance with them. François I, very Christian, will unite with Muslims against Charles V, very Catholic. François I will give money to the Lutherans of Germany to support them in their revolt against the emperor, but, in accordance with custom, he will commence by having Lutherans burnt at home. He pays them in Saxony for political reasons, but in Paris he burns them for political reasons. But what will happen? Persecutions make proselytes? Soon France will be filled with new Protestants. At first they will let themselves be hanged, later will come their turn to hang. There will be civil wars, then will come the Night of St. Bartholomew, then this corner of the world will be worse than all that the ancients and moderns have ever told of hell.

Madmen, who have never been able to give worship to the God who made you! Miscreants, whom the examples of the Noachides, the learned Chinese, the Parseems, and all the sages, have never been able to lead! Monsters, who have need of superstitions as crows' gizzards have need of carrion! You have been told it already, and there remains nothing else to tell you—if you have two religions in your countries, they will cut each other's throat; if you have thirty religions, they will dwell in peace. Look at the great Turk. He governs Guebres, Banians, Greek Christians, Nestorians, Romans. The first who dare to stir up trouble would be impaled. Hence everyone is tranquil.

Of all religions, the Christian is no doubt the one which should inspire tolerance most, although to this point in history the Christians have been the most intolerant of men. The Christian Church was divided in its cradle, and was divided even in the persecutions which under the first emperors it sometimes endured. Often the martyr was regarded as an apostate by his brethren, and the Carpocratian Christian expired be-

neath the sword of the Roman executioners, excommunicated by the Edionite Christian, which in its turn
was anathema to the Sabellian.

This terrible discord, which has lasted for so many
centuries, is a very striking lesson that we should pardon
each other's errors. Discord is the great ill of mankind.
Tolerance is the only remedy for it. . . .

Every sect, as one knows, is a ground of error; there
are no sects of geometers, algebraists, arithmeticians,
because all the propositions of geometry, algebra, and
arithmetic are true. In every other science one may be
deceived. What Thomist or Scotist theologian would dare
say seriously that he is certain of his case?

If it were permitted to reason consistently in religious
matters, it is clear that we all ought to become Jews,
because Jesus Christ our Savior was born a Jew, lived
a Jew, died a Jew, and because he said expressly that
he was accomplishing and fulfilling the Jewish religion.
But it is clearer still that we ought to be tolerant of
one another, because we are all weak, inconsistent,
liable to fickleness and error. Shall a reed laid low in
the mud by the wind say to a fellow reed fallen in the
opposite direction: "Crawl as I crawl, wretch, or I shall
petition that you be torn up by the roots and burned!"

— Reading No. 6 —

BISHOP JOSEPH BUTLER: *THE ANALOGY OF RELIGION, NATURAL AND REVEALED*

The great apologia for religion during the Age of Reason was *The Analogy of Religion, Natural and Revealed,* published in 1737 by Bishop Joseph Butler (1692-1752). Of Presbyterian parentage, Butler joined the Church of England, and became, successively, clerk of the closet to the queen, clerk of the closet to the king, and bishop of Durham. His great work was an indirect attack on the prevailing Deism. It aimed to show that the difficulties raised by the Deists against religion have analogies in nature, for in both realms one finds the limitations of our imperfect human faculties. Bishop Butler regarded religion and nature as a double-edged sword to be employed to defend the Christian faith. Essentially a work of its period, Butler's famous book, in reality, led to skepticism, which rejected both natural religion and revelation as inconsistent and shaky. The following extract is from the conclusion of Butler's book.

✦   ✦   ✦

Whatever account may be given, of the strange in-attention and disregard, in some ages and countries, to a matter of such importance as religion, it would, before experience, be incredible, that there should be the like disregard in those, who have had the moral system of the world laid before them, as it is by Christianity,

and often inculcated upon them, because this moral
system carries in it a good degree and evidence for its
truth, upon its being barely proposed to our thoughts.
There is no need of abstruse understanding, that there
is a God who made and governs the world, and will
judge it in righteousness; though they may be necessary
to answer abstruse difficulties, when once such are raised;
when the very meaning of those words, which express
most intelligibly the general doctrine of religion, is
pretended to be uncertain, and the clear truth of the
thing itself is obscured by the intricacies of speculation.
But, to an unprejudiced mind, ten thousand thousand
instances of design, cannot but prove a Designer. And
it is intuitively manifest, that creatures ought to live
under a dutiful sense of their Maker; and that justice
and charity must be His laws, to creatures when He has
made social, and placed in society.

Indeed, the truth of revealed religion, peculiarly so
called, is not self-evident, but requires external proof,
in order to its being received. Yet inattention, among
us, to revealed religion, will be found to imply the same
dissolute immoral temper of mind, as inattention to
natural religion, because, when both are laid before us,
in the manner they are in Christian countries of liberty,
our obligations to inquire into both, and to embrace
both upon the supposition of their truth, are obligations
of the same nature. . . .

The whole, then, of religion is throughout credible;
nor is there, I think, anything relating to the revealed
dispensation of things more different from the experienced constitution and course of nature, than some parts
of the constitution of nature are from other parts of
it. And if so, the only question which remains is, what
positive evidence can be alleged of the truth of Christianity. This, too, in general, has been considered, and
the objections against it estimated. Deduct, therefore,
what is to be deducted from that evidence upon account
of any weight which may be that to remain in these
objections, after what the analogy of nature has suggested
in answer to them; and then consider what are the
practical consequences from all this, upon the most
skeptical principles one can argue upon (for I am

writing to persons who entertain these principles), and, upon such consideration, it will be obvious, that immorality, as little excuse as it admits of in itself, is greatly aggravated in persons who have been made acquainted with Christianity, whether they believe it or not; because the moral system of nature, or natural religion, which Christianity lays before us, approves itself, almost intuitively, to a reasonable mind, upon seeing it proposed.

In the next place, with regard to Christianity, it will be observed, that there is a middle between a full satisfaction of the truth of it, and a satisfaction of the contrary. The middle state of mind between these two consists in a serious apprehension that it may be true, joined with doubt, whether it be so. And this, upon the best judgment I am able to make, is as far toward speculative infidelity, as any skeptic can at all be supposed to go, who has had true Christianity, with the proper evidence of it, laid before him, and has, in any tolerable measure, considered them.

For I would not be mistaken to comprehend all who have ever heard of it; because it seems evident, that, in many countries called Christian, neither Christianity, nor its evidence, are fairly laid before men. And in such places where both are, there appear to be some who have very little attended to either, and who reject Christianity with a scorn proportionate to their inattention; and yet are by no means without *standing* in other matters. Now it has been shown, that a serious apprehension that Christianity may be true, lays persons under the strictest obligations of a serious regard to it, throughout the whole of their life—a regard not the same exactly, but in many respects nearly the same, with what a full conviction of its truth would lay them under.

Lastly, it will appear, that blasphemy and profaneness, I mean in regard to Christianity, are absolutely without excuse. For there is no temptation to it, but from the wantonness of vanity or mirth; and these, considering the infinite importance of the subject, are no such temptations as to afford any excuse for it. If this be a just account of things, and yet men can go on to vilify or disregard Christianity, which is to talk and act as if they had a demonstration of its falsehood; there is no reason to think they would alter their behavior to any purpose, though there were a demonstration of its truth.

— Reading No. 7 —

THOMAS HOBBES: *LEVIATHAN*

Thomas Hobbes (1588-1679) was born at Westport, the son of a clergyman of the Church of England, and he was educated at Magdalen Hall, Oxford, from which he was graduated in 1608. His political writings caused much comment in his own day, but it was said that his opponents were more conspicuous than his disciples. He exerted a strong influence on Diderot, Spinoza, Leibniz, and Rousseau. "A great partisan of nature," comments one critic, "Hobbes became by the sheer force of his fierce, concentrated intellect a master builder in philosophy. . . . He hated error, and therefore, to refute it, he shouldered his way into the very sanctuary of truth." In 1651 Hobbes published his *Leviathan, or the Matter, Form, and Power of a Commonwealth, Ecclesiastical and Civil,* which appeared in fragment form and strongly influenced political thinking since his day. Dissatisfied with the theory of divine right as a basis for absolutism, Hobbes sought to construct a new science of politics to explain absolutism as a political necessity. These extracts from the opening section of the second part of the *Leviathan* summarize Hobbes' basic ideas on the Commonwealth.

✓   ✓   ✓

*Of the Causes, Generation, and Definition
of a Commonwealth*

The final cause, end, or design of men (who naturally love liberty, and dominion over others) in the introduc-

tion of that restraint upon themselves (in which we see
them live in commonwealths) is the foresight of their
own preservation, and of a more contented life thereby;
that is to say, of getting themselves out of that miserable
condition of war, which is necessarily consequent to the
natural passions of men, when there is no visible power
to keep them in awe, and tie them by fear of punishment
to the performance of their covenants.

For the laws of nature (as *justice, equity, modesty,
mercy,* and [in sum] *doing to others, as we would be
done to*) of themselves, without the terror of some
power, to cause them to be observed, are contrary to
our natural passions. that carry up to partiality, pride,
revenge, and the like. And covenants, without the sword,
are but words, and of no strength to secure a man at
all. Therefore, notwithstanding the laws of nature (which
everyone hath then kept, when he has the will to keep
them, when he can do it safely) if there be no power
erected, or not great enough for our security; every man
will, and may lawfully rely on his own strength and art,
for caution against all other men. And in all places,
where men have lived by small families, to rob and
spoil one another, has been a trade, and so far from being
reputed against the law of nature, that the greater spoils
they gained, the greater was their honor; and men observed no other laws therein, but the laws of honor;
that is, to abstain from cruelty, leaving to men their
lives, and instruments of husbandry. And as small
families did then; so now do cities and kingdoms, which
are but greater families (for their own security) enlarge their dominions, upon all pretences of danger, and
fear of invasion, or assistance that may be given to
invaders, endeavor as much as they can, to subdue, or
weaken their neighbors, by open force, and secret arts,
for want of other caution, justly; and are remembered for
it in after ages with honor.

Nor is it the joining together of a small number of
men, that gives them this security; because in small
numbers, small additions on the one side or the other,
make the advantage of strength so great, as is sufficient
to carry the victory; and therefore gives encouragement
to an invasion. The multitude sufficient to confide in

for our security, is not determined by any certain number, but by comparison with the enemy we fear; and is then sufficient, when the odds of the enemy is not of so visible and conspicuous moment, to determine in the event of war, as to move him to attempt. . . .

It is true that certain living creatures, as bees and ants, live sociably with one another (which are therefore by Aristotle numbered amongst political creatures); and yet have no other direction, than their particular judgments and appetites; nor speech, whereby one of them can signify to another, what he thinks expedient for the common benefit: and therefore some man may perhaps desire to know, why mankind cannot do the same. To which I answer:

First, that men are continually in competition for honor and dignity, which these creatures are not; and consequently amongst men there arises on that ground, envy and hatred, and finally war; but amongst these not so.

Secondly, that amongst these creatures, the common good differs not from the private; and being by nature inclined to their private, they procure thereby the common benefit. But man, whose joy consists in comparing himself with other men, can relish nothing but what is eminent.

Thirdly, that these creatures, having not (as man) the use of reason, do not see, nor think they see any fault, in the administration of their common business: whereas among men, there are very many that think themselves wiser, and abler to govern the public, better than the rest; and these strive to reform and innovate, one this way, another that way; and thereby bring it into distraction and civil war.

Fourthly, that these creatures, though they have some use of voice in making known to one another their desires, and other affections; yet they want that art of words, by which some men can represent to others, that which is good, in the likeness of evil; and evil, in the likeness of good; and augment, or diminish the apparent greatness of good and evil; discontenting men, and troubling their peace at their pleasure.

Fifthly, irrational creatures cannot distinguish be-

tween *injury* and *damage;* and therefore as long as they
be at ease, they are not offended with their fellows:
whereas man is then most troublesome, when he is
most at ease: for then it is that he loves to show his
wisdom, and control the actions of them that govern
the Commonwealth.

Lastly, the agreement of these creatures is natural;
that of men, is by covenant only, which is artificial: and
therefore it is no wonder if there be somewhat else
required (besides covenant) to make their agreement
constant and lasting; which is a common power, to keep
them in awe, and to direct their action to the common
benefit.

The only way to erect such a common power, as may
be able to defend them from the invasion of foreigners,
and the injuries of one another, and thereby to secure
them in such sort, as that by their own industry, and by
the fruits of the earth, they may nourish themselves and
live contentedly; is, to confer all their power and strength
upon one man, or upon one assembly of men, that may
reduce all their wills, by plurality of voices, unto one
will: which is as much as to say, to appoint one man,
or assembly of men, to bear their persons; and everyone
to own, and acknowledge himself to be author of whatsoever he that so beareth their person, shall act, or
cause to be acted, in those things which concern the
common peace and safety; and therein to submit their
wills, every one to his will, and their judgments, to his
judgment. This is more than consent, or concord; it is
a real unity of them all, in one and the same person,
made by covenant of every man with every man, in
such manner, as if every man should say to every man,
*I authorize and give up my right of governing myself,
to this man, or to this assembly of men, on this condition, that thou give up thy right to him, and authorize
all his actions in like manner.*

This done, the multitude so united in one person, is
called a Commonwealth, in Latin *Civitas.* This is the
generation of that great Leviathan, or rather (to speak
more reverently) of that mortal God, to which we owe
under the immortal God, our peace and defence. For
by this authority, given him by every particular man in

the Commonwealth, he has the use of so much power and strength conferred on him, that by terror thereof, he is enabled to form the wills of them all, to peace at home, and mutual aid against their enemies abroad. And in him consists the essence of the Commonwealth; which (to define it) *is one person, of whose acts a great multitude by mutual covenants one with another, have made themselves every one the author, to the end he may use the strength and means of them all, as he shall think expedient for their peace and common defence.*

And he that carries this person, is called *sovereign,* and said to have *sovereign power;* and every one besides his *subject.*

The attaining of this sovereign power is by two ways. One, by natural force; as when a man makes his children to submit themselves and their children to his government, as being able to destroy them if they refuse; or by war subdues his enemies to his will, giving them their lives on that condition. The other is when men agree amongst themselves to submit to some man, or assembly of men, voluntarily, on confidence to be protected by him against all others. This latter may be called a political Commonwealth, or Commonwealth by *institution;* and the former a Commonwealth by *acquisition.*

— Reading No. 8 —

JOHN LOCKE: *AN ESSAY CONCERNING HUMAN UNDERSTANDING*

John Locke (1632-1704), the son of a Puritan soldier in the English civil war, was born near Bristol, England, and was educated at Westminster School, where Dryden was his contemporary, and at Christ Church, Oxford. His study of Descartes first gave him "a relish of philosophical things." In 1690 Locke published a small work with an unassuming title: *An Essay Concerning Human Understanding,* whose immediate effects were revolutionary. The essay was widely hailed as the first attempt in modern times to arrive at a comprehensive theory of knowledge. Locke became a symbol of the true philosopher who rejects vague and contradictory systems in favor of constant contact with reality. The following extracts from Locke's famous essay explain his aims and his thoughts on ideas in general.

✓   ✓   ✓

Introduction

1. *An inquiry into the understanding, pleasant and useful.*—Since it is the understanding that sets man above the rest of sensible beings, and gives him all the advantage and dominion which he has over them, it is certainly a subject, even for its nobleness, worth our labor to inquire into. The understanding, like the eye,

whilst it makes us see and perceive all other things, takes no notice of itself; and it requires art and pains to set it at a distance, and make it its own object. But whatever be the difficulties that lie in the way of this inquiry, whatever it be that keeps us so much in the dark to ourselves, sure I am that all the light we can let in upon our own minds, all the acquaintance we can make with our own understandings, will not only be very pleasant, but bring us great advantage in directing our thoughts in the search of other things.

2. *Design.*—This therefore being my purpose, to inquire into the original, certainty, and extent of human knowledge, together with the grounds and degrees of belief, opinion, and assent, I shall not at present meddle with the physical consideration of the mind, or trouble to examine wherein its essence consists, or by what motions of our spirits, or alterations of our bodies, we come to have any sensation by our organs, or by any ideas in our understandings; and whether those ideas do, in their formation, any or all of them, depend on matter or no: these are speculations which, however curious and entertaining, I shall decline, as lying out of my way in the design I am now upon. It shall suffice to my present purpose, to consider the discerning faculties of a man as they are employed about the objects which they have to do with; and I shall imagine I have not wholly misemployed myself in the thoughts I shall have on this occasion, if, in this historical, plain method, I can give any account of the ways whereby our understandings come to attain those notions of things we have. . . .

3. *Method.*—It is therefore worth while to search out the bounds between opinion and knowledge, and examine by what measures, in things whereof we have no certain knowledge, we ought to regulate our assent, and moderate our persuasions. In order whereunto, I shall pursue this following method:—

First: I shall inquire into the original of those ideas, notions, or whatever else you please to call them, which a man observes, and is conscious to himself he has in mind, and the ways whereby the understanding comes to be furnished with them.

Secondly: I shall endeavor to show what knowledge the understanding hath by those ideas, and the certainty, evidence, and extent of it.

Thirdly: I shall make some inquiry into the nature and grounds of faith or opinion; whereby I mean, that assent which we give to any proposition as true, of whose truth yet we have no certain knowledge: and here we shall have occasion to examine the reasons and degrees of assent. . . .

6. *Knowledge of our capacity a cure of skepticism and idleness.*—When we know our own strength, we shall the better know what to undertake with hopes of success; and when we have well surveyed the powers of our own minds, and made some estimate what we may expect from them, we shall not be inclined either to sit still, and not set our thoughts on work at all, in despair of knowing anything; nor, on the other side, question everything, and disclaim all knowledge, because some things are not to be understood. It is of great use to the sailor to know the length of his line, though he cannot with it fathom all the depths of the ocean; it is well he knows that it is long enough to reach the bottom at such places as are necessary to direct his voyage, and caution him against running upon shoals that may ruin him. Our business here is not to know all things, but those which concern our conduct. If we can find out those measures whereby a rational creature, put in that state which man is in this world, may and ought to govern his opinions and actions depending thereon, we need not be troubled that some other things escape our knowledge. . . .

Of Ideas in General, and Their Original

1. *Idea is the object of thinking.*—Every man being conscious to himself, that he thinks, and that which his mind is applied about, whilst thinking, being the ideas that are there, it is past doubt that men have in their mind several ideas, such as are those expressed by the words, "whiteness, hardness, sweetness, thinking, motion, man, elephant, army, drunkenness," and others. It is in the first place then to be inquired, how he comes by them? I know it is a received doctrine, that men have

native ideas and original characters stamped upon their minds in their very first being. . . .

2. *All ideas come from sensation or reflection.*—Let us then suppose the mind to be, as we say, white paper (*tabula rasa*), void of all characters, without any ideas; how comes it to be furnished? Whence comes it by that vast store, which the busy and boundless fancy of man has painted on it with an almost endless variety? Whence has it all the materials of reason and knowledge? To this I answer, in one word, from EXPERIENCE: in that all our knowledge is founded, and from that it ultimately derives itself. Our observation, employed either about external sensible objects, or about the internal operations of our minds, perceived and reflected on by ourselves, is that which supplies our understandings with all the *materials* of thinking. These two are the fountain of knowledge, from whence all the ideas we have, or can naturally have, do spring.

3. *The object of sensation one source of ideas.*— First: Our senses, conversant about particular sensible objects, do convey into the mind several distinct perceptions of things, according to those various ways wherein those objects do affect them; and thus we come by those ideas we have of yellow, white, heat, cold, soft, hard, bitter, sweet, and all those which we call sensible qualities; which when I say the senses convey into the mind, I mean, they from external objects convey into the mind what produces there those perceptions. This great source of most of the ideas we have, depending wholly upon our senses, and derived by them to the understanding, I call "sensation."

4. *The operations of our minds the other source of them.*—Secondly: The other fountain, from which experience furnisheth the understanding with ideas, is the perception of the operations of our own minds within us, as it is employed about the ideas it has got; which operations, when the soul comes to reflect on and consider, do furnish the understanding with another set of ideas which could not be had from things without; and such are perception, thinking, doubting, believing, reasoning, knowing, willing, and all the different actings

of our own minds; which we, being conscious of, and observing in ourselves, do from these receive into our understanding as distinct ideas, as we do from bodies affecting our senses. This source of ideas every man has wholly in himself; and though it be not sense as having nothing to do with external objects, yet it is very like it, and might properly enough be called "internal sense." But as I call the other "sensation," so I call this "reflection," the ideas it affords being such only as the mind gets by reflecting on its own operations within itself. . . .

5. *All our ideas are of the one or the other of these.*— The understanding seems to me not to have the least glimmering of any ideas which it doth not receive from one of these two. External objects furnish the mind with the ideas of sensible qualities, which are all those different perceptions they produce in us; and the mind furnishes the understanding with ideas of its own operation.

These . . . contain our whole stock of ideas; and we have nothing in our minds which did not come in one of these two ways. Let any one examine his own thoughts, and thoroughly search into his understanding, and then let him tell me, whether all the original ideas he has there, are any other than of the objects of his senses, or of the operation of his mind considered as objects of his reflection; and how great a mass of knowledge soever he imagines to be lodged there, he will, upon taking a strict view, see that he has not any idea in his mind but what one of these two hath imprinted, though perhaps with infinite variety compounded and enlarged by the understanding. . . .

— Reading No. 9 —

BERKELEY: *THE PRINCIPLES OF HUMAN KNOWLEDGE*

George Berkeley (1685-1753), Bishop of Cloyne, was born in the County of Kilkenny, Ireland, and was educated at Trinity College, Dublin, where he became deeply interested in the new philosophy of Locke, in contrast to the old scholasticism. In 1710, at the age of twenty-five, Berkeley published his *Treatise Concerning the Principles of Human Knowledge*. The progress of scientific discovery and the consequent importance attached to those aspects of the world, with which scientific method was equipped to deal, had tended to promote the rise of skepticism and atheism. Berkeley sought, in opposition to the skeptics and atheists, to open a method for rendering the sciences more easy, useful, and compendious, to demonstrate the reality and perfection of human knowledge, the incorporeal nature of the soul, and the immediate providence of a Deity.

✓   ✓   ✓

1. It is evident to anyone who takes a survey of the objects of human knowledge, that they are either ideas (1) actually imprinted on the senses, or else such as are (2) perceived by attending to the passions and operations of the mind, or lastly (3) ideas formed by help of memory and imagination, either compounding, dividing, or barely representing those originally perceived in the aforesaid ways. By sight I have the ideas of lights and colors, with their several degrees and variations. By

touch I perceive hard and soft, heat and cold, motion and resistance, and of all these more and less either as to quantity or degree. Smelling furnishes me with odors, the palate with tastes, and hearing conveys sounds to the mind in all their variety of tone and composition. And as several of these are observed to accompany each other, they came to be marked by one name, and so to be reputed as one thing. Thus, for example, a certain color, taste, smell, figure, and consistence, having been observed to go together, are accounted one distinct thing, as signified by the name—"apple." Other collections of ideas constitute a stone, a tree, a book, and the like sensible things; which, as they are pleasing or disagreeable, excite the passions of love, hatred, joy, grief, and so forth.

2. But besides all that endless variety of ideas or objects of knowledge, there is likewise something which knows or perceives them, and exercises diverse operations, as willing, imagining, remembering, about them. This perceiving, active being is what I call *mind, spirit, soul,* or *myself.* By which words I do not denote any one of my ideas, but a thing entirely distinct from them wherein they exist, or, which is the same thing, whereby they are perceived; for the existence of an idea consists in being perceived.

3. That neither our thoughts, nor passions, for ideas formed by the imagination, exist without the mind, is what everybody will allow. And it seems no less evident that the various sensations or ideas imprinted on the sense, however blended or combined together (that is, whatever objects they compose), cannot exist otherwise than in a mind perceiving them. I think an intuitive knowledge may be obtained of this by anyone that shall attend to what is meant by the term "exist" when applied to sensible things. The table I write on I say exists—that is, I see and feel it; and if I were out of my study I should say it existed—meaning thereby that if I was in my study I might perceive it, or that some other spirit actually does perceive it. There was an odor, that is, it was smelt; there is a sound, that is, it was heard; a color or figure, and it was perceived by sight or touch. This is all that I can understand by these and the like expres-

sions. For as to what is said of the absolute existence of
unthinking things without any relation to their being
perceived, that seems perfectly unintelligible. Their *esse*
is *percipi*, nor is it possible they should have any existence out of the minds or thinking things which perceive
them.

4. It is indeed an opinion strangely prevailing amongst
men, that houses, mountains, rivers, and in a word all
sensible objects, have an existence, natural or real, distinct from their being perceived by the understanding.
But with how great an assurance and acquiescence
soever this principle may be entertained in the world,
yet whoever shall find in his heart to call it in question
may, if I mistake not, perceive it to involve a manifest
contradiction. For what are the aforementioned objects
but the things we perceive by sense? and what do we
perceive *besides our own ideas or sensations?* and is it
not plainly repugnant that any one of these, or any combination of them, should exist unperceived?

5. If we thoroughly examine this tenet it will perhaps
be found at bottom to depend on the doctrine of *abstract
ideas*. For can there be a nicer strain of abstraction than
to distinguish the existence of sensible objects from their
being perceived, so as to conceive them existing unperceived? Light and colors, heat and cold, extension and
figures—in a word the things we see and feel—what are
they but so many sensations, notions, ideas, or impressions on the sense? And is it possible to separate, even
in thought, any of these from perception? For my part,
I might as easily divide a thing from itself. I may, indeed, divide in my thoughts, or conceive apart from each
other, those things which perhaps I never perceived by
sense so divided. Thus I imagine the trunk of a human
body without the limbs, or conceive the smell of a rose
without thinking on the rose itself. So far, I will not
deny, I can abstract, if that may properly be called abstraction which extends only to the conceiving separately
such objects as it is possible may really exist or be actually perceived asunder. But my conceiving or imagining
power does not extend beyond the possibility of real
existence or perception. Hence, as it is impossible for
me to see or feel anything without an actual sensation

of that thing, so it is impossible for me to conceive in
my thoughts any sensible thing or object distinct from
the sensation or perception of it. . . .

8. But, say you, though the ideas themselves do not
exist without the mind, yet there may be things *like*
them, whereof they are copies or resemblances, which
things exist without the mind in an unthinking substance.
I answer, an idea can be like nothing but an idea; a
color figure can be like nothing but another color figure.
If we look but never so little into our thoughts, we shall
find it impossible for us to conceive a likeness except
only between our ideas. Again, I ask whether those supposed originals or external things, of which our ideas are
the pictures or representations, be themselves perceivable
or no? If they are, then they are ideas and we have
gained our point; but if you say they are not, I appeal
to any one whether it be sense to assert a color is like
something which is invisible; hard or soft, like something which is intangible; and so of the rest. . . .

22. I am afraid that I have given cause to think I am
needlessly prolix in handling this subject. For, to what
purpose is it to dilate on that which may be demonstrated with the utmost evidence in a line or two, to
anyone that is capable of the least reflection? It is but
looking into your own thoughts, and so trying whether
you can conceive it possible for a sound, or figure, or
motion, or color to exist without the mind or unperceived. This easy trial may perhaps make you see that
what you contend for is a downright contradiction. Inso-
much that I am content to put the whole upon this issue:
if you can but conceive it possible for one extended
movable substance, or, in general, for any one idea, or
anything like an idea, to exist otherwise than in a mind
perceiving it, I shall readily give up the cause; and, as
for all that compages of external bodies you contend
for, I shall grant you its existence, though you cannot
either give me any reason why you believe it exists, or
assign any use to it when it is supposed to exist. I say,
the bare possibility of your opinions being true shall
pass for an argument that it is so.

— Reading No. 10 —

CONDORCET: *PROGRESS OF THE HUMAN MIND*

Marie Jean Antoine Nicolas Caritat, Marquis de Condorcet (1743-1794), was born in Picardy, and educated at the Jesuit College in Rheims and at the College of Navarre in Paris. A zealous propagandist for the religious and political views of the *philosophes,* he greeted the outbreak of the French Revolution with enthusiasm, and was one of the first to declare for a republic. His best-known work, *Outlines of an Historical View of the Progress of the Human Mind,* projected the idea of the continuous progress of the human race to perfection, and the equality of civil and political rights for both sexes. He attributed the excesses of the Revolution to bad institutions, from which humanity would ultimately free itself. His book was the ideal expression of the supreme optimism and confidence of the thinkers of the Age of Reason. Imprisoned at Bourg-la-Reine for his political views, he was found dead in his cell, whether from poison or exhaustion is unknown.

✓   ✓   ✓

All the causes which contribute to the improvement of the human species . . . must, from their very nature, exercise an influence always active, and acquire an extent forever increasing. The proofs of this have been exhibited, and from their development in the work itself they will derive additional force: accordingly we may already conclude, that the perfectibility of man is in-

definite. Meanwhile we have hitherto considered him as
possessing only the same natural faculties, as endowed
with the same organization. How much greater would
be the certainty, how much wider the compass of our
hopes, could we prove that these natural faculties themselves, that this very organization, are also susceptible of
amelioration? And this is the last question that we shall
examine.

The organic perfectibility or deterioration of the
classes of the vegetable, or species of the animal kingdom, may be regarded as one of the general laws of
nature.

This law extends to the human race; and it cannot be
doubted that the progress of the sanitative art [sanita-
tion], that the use of more wholesome food and more
comfortable habitations, that a mode of life which shall
develop the physical powers by exercise, without at the
same time impairing them by excess; in fine, that the
destruction of the two most active causes of deterioration, penury and wretchedness on the one hand, and
enormous wealth on the other, must necessarily tend to
prolong the common duration of man's existence, and
secure him a more constant health and a more robust
constitution. It is manifest that the improvement of the
practice of medicine, become more efficacious in consequence of the progress of reason and the social order,
must in the end put a period to transmissible or contagious disorders, as well to those general maladies resulting from climate, ailments, and the nature of certain
occupations. Nor would it be difficult to prove that this
hope might be extended to almost every other malady,
of which it is probable we shall hereafter discover the
most remote causes. Would it even be absurd to suppose
this quality of melioration in the human species as susceptible of an indefinite advancement; to suppose that a
period must one day arrive when death will be nothing
more than the effect either of extraordinary accidents, or
of the flow and gradual decay of the vital powers; and
that the duration of the middle space, of the interval
between the birth of man and this decay, will itself have
no assignable limit? Certainly man will not become immortal; but may not the distance between the moment

in which he draws his first breath and the common term when, in the course of nature, without malady, without accident, he finds it impossible any longer to exist, be necessarily protracted? As we are now speaking of a progress that is capable of being represented with precision, by numerical quantities or by lines, we shall embrace the opportunity of explaining the two meanings that may be affixed to the word *indefinite*.

In reality, this middle term of life, which in proportion as men advance upon the ocean of futurity, we have supposed incessantly to increase, may receive additions either in conformity to a law by which, though approaching continually an illimitable extent, it could never possibly arrive at it; or a law by which, in the immensity of ages, it may acquire a greater extent than any determinate quantity whatever that may be assigned as its limit. In the latter case, this duration of life is indefinite in the strictest sense of the word, since there exist no bounds on this side of which it must necessarily stop. And in the former, it is equally indefinite to us; if we cannot fix the term, it may forever approach, but can never surpass; particularly if, knowing only that it can never stop, we are ignorant in which of the two senses the term indefinite is applicable to it; and this is precisely the state of the knowledge we have as yet acquired relative to the perfectibility of the species.

Thus, in the instance we are considering, we are bound to believe that the mean duration of human life will forever increase, unless its increase can be prevented by the physical revolutions of the system: but we cannot tell what is the bound which the duration of human life can never exceed; we cannot even tell, whether there be any circumstance in the laws of nature which has determined and laid down its limit.

But may not our physical faculties, the force, the sagacity, the acuteness of the senses, be numbered among the qualities, the individual improvement of which it will be practicable to transmit? An attention to the different breeds of animals must lead us to adopt the affirmative of this question, and a direct observation of the human species itself will be found to strengthen the opinion.

Lastly, may we not include in the same circle the intellectual and moral faculties? May not our parents, who transmit to us the advantages or defects of their conformation, and from whom we received our features and shape, as well as our propensities to certain physical affections, transmit to us also that part of organization upon which intellect, strength of understanding, energy of soul or moral sensibility depend? Is it not probable that education, by improving these qualities will at the same time have an influence upon, will modify and improve this organization itself? Analogy, an investigation of the human faculties, and even some facts, appear to authorize these conjectures, and thereby to enlarge the boundary of our hopes.

Such are the questions with which we shall terminate the last division of our work. And how admirably calculated is this view of the human race, emancipated from its chains, released alike from the dominion of chance, as well as from that of the enemies of its progress, and advancing with a firm and indeviate step in the paths of truth, to console the philosopher lamenting the errors, the flagrant acts of injustice, the crimes with which the earth is still polluted? It is the contemplation of this prospect that rewards him for all his efforts to assist the progress of reason and the establishment of liberty. He dares to regard these efforts as a part of the eternal chain of the destiny of mankind; and in this persuasion he finds the true delight of virtue, the pleasure of having performed a durable service, which no vicissitude will ever destroy in a fatal operation calculated to restore the reign of prejudice and slavery. This sentiment is the asylum into which he retires, and to which the memory of his persecutors cannot follow him: he unites himself in imagination with man restored to his rights, delivered from oppression, and proceeding with rapid strides in the path of happiness: he forgets his own misfortunes while his thoughts are thus employed; he lives no longer to adversity, calumny, and malice, but becomes the associate of these wiser and more fortunate beings whose enviable condition he so earnestly contributed to produce.

— Reading No. 11 —

ADAM SMITH: *THE WEALTH OF NATIONS*

Adam Smith (1723-1790) was born at Kirkcaldy, Scotland, and was educated at Glasgow University and finally at Balliol College, Oxford, where he studied for seven years. In 1751 he became professor of logic at Glasgow University and the next year professor of moral philosophy. In 1776 he published his famous *An Inquiry into the Nature and Causes of the Wealth of Nations,* which won immediate recognition and established his permanent reputation. Adam Smith had a vast influence not only on economics but also on practical politics. His spirited defence of free trade and his indictment of the East India Company strongly affected the course of British history. His prestige was further manifested in the reform of the British commercial system by the repeal of the Corn Laws and the Navigation Laws.

✓　　　✓　　　✓

Of the Principle of the Commercial or Mercantile System

That wealth consists in money, or in gold and silver, is a popular notion which naturally arises from the double function of money, as the instrument of commerce, and as the measure of value. In consequence of its being the instrument of commerce, when we have money we can more readily obtain whatever else we have occasion for, than by means of any other commodity. The great affair, we always find, is to get money.

When that is obtained, there is no difficulty in making any subsequent purchase. In consequence of its being the measure of value, we estimate that of all other commodities by the quantities of money which they will exchange for. We say of a rich man that he is worth a great deal, and of a poor man that he is worth very little money. A frugal man, or a man eager to be rich, is said to love money; and a careless, a generous, or a profuse man, is said to be indifferent about it. To grow rich is to get money; and wealth and money, in short, are, in common language, considered as in every respect synonymous.

A rich country, in the same manner as a rich man, is supposed to be a country abounding in money; and to heap up gold and silver in any country is supposed to be the readiest way to enrich it. For some time after the discovery of America, the first inquiry of the Spaniards, when they arrived upon any unknown coast, used to be, if there was any gold or silver to be found in the neighborhood? For the information which they received, they judged whether it was worth while to make a settlement there, or if the country was worth the conquering. Plano Carpino, a monk sent ambassador from the king of France to one of the sons of the famous Gengis Khan, says that the Tartars used frequently to ask him, if there was plenty of sheep and oxen in the kingdom of France? Their inquiry had the same object with that of the Spaniards. They wanted to know if the country was rich enough to be worth the conquering. . . .

Mr. Locke remarks a distinction between money and other moveable goods. All other moveable goods, he says, are of so consumable a nature that the wealth which consists in them cannot be much depended on, and a nation which abounds in them one year may, without any exportation, but merely by their own waste and extravagance, be in great want of them the next. Money, on the contrary, is a steady friend, which, though it may travel about from hand to hand, yet if it can be kept from going out of the country, is not very liable to be wasted or consumed. Gold and silver, therefore, are, according to him, the most solid and substantial part of the moveable wealth of a nation, and to multiply those metals ought, he thinks, upon that account, to be the great object of its political economy.

Others admit that if a nation could be separated from all the world, it would be of no consequence how much, or how little money accumulated in it. The consumable goods which were circulated by means of this money, would only be exchanged for a greater or a smaller number of pieces; but the real wealth or poverty of the country, they allow, would depend altogether upon the abundance or scarcity of those consumable goods. But it is otherwise, they think, with countries which have connections with foreign nations, and which are obliged to carry on foreign wars, and to maintain fleets and armies in distant countries. This, they say, cannot be done, but by sending abroad money to pay them with; and a nation cannot send much money abroad, unless it has a good deal at home. Every such nation, therefore, must endeavor in time of peace to accumulate gold and silver, that, when occasion requires, it may have wherewithal to carry on foreign wars.

In consequence of these popular notions, all the different nations of Europe have studied, though to little purpose, every possible means of accumulating gold and silver in their respective countries. . . .

It would be too ridiculous to go about seriously to prove, that wealth does not consist in money, or in gold and silver; but in what money purchases, and is valuable only for purchasing. Money, no doubt, makes always a part of the national capital; but it has already been shown that it generally takes but a small part, and always the most unprofitable part of it. . . .

It is not always necessary to accumulate gold and silver, in order to enable a country to carry on foreign wars, and to maintain fleets and armies in distant countries. Fleets and armies are maintained, not with gold and silver, but with consumable goods. The nation which, from the annual produce of its domestic industry, from the annual revenue arising out of its lands, labor, and consumable stock, has wherewithal to purchase those consumable goods in distant countries, can maintain foreign wars there. . . .

Though the encouragement of exportation and the

discouragement of importation, are the two great engines
by which the mercantile system proposes to enrich every
country, yet with regard to some particular commodities,
it seems to follow an opposite plan: to discourage exportation and to encourage importation. Its ultimate
object, however, it pretends, is always the same, to enrich the country by an advantageous balance of trade.
It discourages the exportation of the materials of manufacture, and of the instruments of trade, in order to give
our own workmen an advantage, and to enable them to
undersell those of other nations in all foreign markets:
and by restraining, in this manner, the exportation of a
few commodities, of no great price, it proposes to occasion a much greater and more valuable exportation of
others. It encourages the importation of the materials of
manufacture, in order that our own people may be enabled to work them up more cheaply, and thereby prevent a greater and more valuable importation of the
manufactured commodities. . . .

Consumption is the sole end and purpose of all production; and the interest of the producer ought to be
attended to, only so far as it may be necessary for pro-
moting that of the consumer. The maxim is so perfectly
self-evident, that it would be absurd to attempt to prove
it. But in the mercantile system, the interest of the consumer is always constantly sacrificed to that of the producer; and it seems to consider production, and not
consumption, as the ultimate end and object of all industry and commerce.

In the restraints upon the importation of all foreign
commodities which can come into competition with
those of our own growth, or manufacture, the interest
of the home-consumer is evidently sacrificed to that of
the producer. It is altogether for the benefit of the latter,
that the former is obliged to pay that enhancement of
price which this monopoly almost always occasions.

It is altogether for the benefit of the producer that
bounties are granted upon the exportation of some of his
productions. The home-consumer is obliged to pay, first,
the tax which is necessary for paying the bounty, and
secondly, the still greater tax which necessarily arises

from the enhancement of the price of the commodity in the home market. . . .

It cannot be very difficult to determine who have been the contrivers of this whole mercantile system; not the consumers, we may believe, whose interest has been entirely neglected; but the producers, whose interest has been so carefully attended to; and among this latter class our merchants and manufacturers have been by far the principal architects. In the mercantile regulations, the interest of our manufacturers has been most peculiarly attended to; and the interest, not so much of the consumers, as that of some other sets of producers, has been sacrificed to it.

The agricultural systems of political economy, which represents the produce of land as the sole source of the revenue and wealth of every country has, so far as I know, never been adopted by any nation, and it at present exists only in the speculations of a few men of great learning and ingenuity in France. It would not, surely, be worth while to examine at great length the errors of a system which never has done, and probably never will do any harm in any part of the world.

— Reading No. 12 —

T. R. MALTHUS: *AN ESSAY ON THE PRINCIPLE OF POPULATION*

Thomas Robert Malthus (1766-1834) was born in Surrey, England, educated at Jesus College, Cambridge, was ordained, and became professor of modern history in the East India Company's College at Haileybury. His great work, *An Essay on the Principle of Population as it Affects the Future Improvement of Society,* was first published anonymously in 1798. A few years later it appeared under his name The Rev. T. R. Malthus, A.M. F.R.S., with the extraordinary title: *An Essay on the Principle of Population or, a View of its Past and Present Effects on Human Happiness; with an Inquiry into our Prospects Respecting the Future Removal or Mitigation of the Evils which it Occasions.* Malthus' conclusion that population is necessarily limited by the checks of vice and misery aroused a storm of criticism and abuse.

✓   ✓   ✓

In an inquiry concerning the improvement of society, the mode of conducting the subject which naturally presents itself, is,

1. To investigate the causes that have hitherto impeded the progress of mankind towards happiness; and,

2. To examine the probability of the total or partial removal of these causes in future.

To enter fully into this question, and to enumerate all the causes that have hitherto influenced human improvement, would be much beyond the power of an individual. The principal object of the present essay is to examine the effects of one great cause intimately united with the very nature of man; which, though it has been constantly and powerfully operating since the commencement of society, has been little noticed by the writers who have treated this subject. The facts which establish the existence of this cause have, indeed, been repeatedly stated and acknowledged; but its most natural and necessary effects have been almost totally overlooked; though probably among these effects may be reckoned a very considerable portion of that vice and misery, and of that unequal distribution of the bounties of nature, which it has been the unceasing object of the enlightened philanthropist in all ages to correct.

The cause to which I allude, is the constant tendency in all animated life to increase beyond the nourishment prepared for it.

It is observed by Dr. Franklin, there is no bound to the prolific nature of plants or animals, but what is made by their crowding and interfering with each other's means of subsistence. Were the face of the earth, he says, vacant of other plants, it might be gradually sowed and overspread with one kind only, as for instance with fennel: and were it empty of other inhabitants, it might in a few ages be replenished from one nation, as for instance with Englishmen.

This is incontrovertibly true. Through the animal and vegetable kingdom Nature has scattered the seeds of life abroad with the most profuse and liberal hand; but has been comparatively sparing in the room and the nourishment necessary to rear them. The germs of existence contained in this earth, if they could freely develop themselves, would fill millions of worlds in the course of a few thousand years. Necessity, that imperious, all-pervading law of nature, restrains them within the prescribed bounds. The race of plants and the race of animals shrink under this great restrictive law; and man cannot by any efforts of reason escape from it.

In plants and irrational animals, the view of the subject is simple. They are all impelled by a powerful instinct to the increase of their species; and this instinct is interrupted by no doubts about providing for their offspring. Wherever therefore there is liberty, the power of increase is exerted; and the superabundant effects are repressed afterwards by want of room and nourishment.

The effects of this check on man are more complicated. Impelled to the increase of his species by an equally powerful instinct, reason interrupts his career, and asks him whether he may not bring beings into the world, for whom he cannot provide the means of support. If he attend to this natural suggestion, the restriction too frequently produces vice. If he hear not, the human race will be constantly endeavoring to increase beyond the means of subsistence. But as, by that law of our nature which makes food necessary to the life of man, population can never actually increase beyond the lowest nourishment capable of supporting it, a strong check on population, from the difficulty of acquiring food, must be constantly in operation. This difficulty must fall somewhere, and must necessarily be severely felt in some or other of the various forms of misery, or the fear of misery, by a large portion of mankind. . . .

It may safely be pronounced that the population, when unchecked, goes on doubling itself every twenty-five years, or increases in a geometrical ratio.

The rate according to which the productions of the earth may be supposed to increase, it will not be so easy to determine. Of this, however, we may be perfectly certain, that the ratio of their increase in a limited territory must be of a totally different nature from the ratio of the increase of population. A thousand millions are just as easily doubled every twenty-five years by the power of population as a thousand. But the food to support the increase from the greater number will by no means be obtained with the same facility. Man is necessarily confined in room. When acre has been added to acre till all the fertile land is occupied, the yearly increase of food must depend upon the melioration of the land already in possession. This is a fund, which, from the nature of all soils, instead of increasing, must be gradually diminishing. But population, could it be supplied with food, would go on with unexhausted vigor; and the increase of one period would furnish the power of a greater increase the next, and this without any limit. . . .

It may be fairly pronounced, therefore, that, considering the present average state of the earth, the means of subsistence, under circumstances the most favorable to human industry, could not possibly be made to increase faster than in an arithmetical ratio.

The necessary effects of these two different rates of increase, when brought together, will be very striking. Let us call the population of this island eleven millions; and suppose the present produce equal to the easy support of such a number. In the first twenty-five years the population would be twenty-two millions, and the food being also doubled, the means of subsistence would be equal to this increase. In the next twenty-five years, the population would be forty-four millions, and the means of subsistence only equal to the support of thirty-three millions. In the next period the population would be eighty-eight millions, and the means of subsistence just equal to the support of half that number. And, at the conclusion of the first century, the population would be a hundred and seventy-six millions, and the means of subsistence only equal to the support of fifty-five millions, leaving a population of a hundred and twenty-five millions totally unprovided for.

Taking the whole earth, instead of this island, emigration would of course be excluded; and, supposing the present population equal to a thousand millions, the human species would increase as the numbers 1,2,4,8,16, 32,64,128,256, and subsistence as 1,2,3,4,5,6,7,8,9. In two centuries the population would be to the means of subsistence as 256 to 9; in three centuries as 4096 to 13; and in two thousand years the difference would be almost incalculable.

In this supposition no limits whatever are placed to the produce of the earth. It may increase forever and be greater than an assignable quantity; yet still the power of population being in every period so much superior, the increase of the human species can only be kept down to the level of the means of subsistence by the constant operation of the strong law of necessity, acting as a check upon the greater power. . . .

The ultimate check to population appears then to be a want of food, arising necessarily from the different ratios according to the population and food increase. But this ultimate check is never the immediate check, except in cases of actual famine.

The immediate check may be stated to consist in all those customs, and all those diseases, which seem to be generated by a scarcity of the means of subsistence; and all those causes, independent of this scarcity, whether of a moral or physical nature, which tend prematurely to weaken and destroy the human frame. . . .

On examining these obstacles to the increase of population, which I have classed under the heads of preventive checks, it will appear that they are all resolvable into moral restraint, vice, and misery.

·— Reading No. 13 —

DAVID RICARDO: *THE PRINCIPLES OF POLITICAL ECONOMY AND TAXATION*

David Ricardo (1772-1823), an English political economist, gave his name to a system and method known as Ricardoan economics. His chief work, entitled *The Principles of Political Economy and Taxation* (1817), remarkable for its purely deductive method, brought about what amounted to a revolution in political economy. "This was a work in many respects far from original," says F. W. Kolthammer, "an outcome of much friendly discussion and private mental concentration, which its author published only with the greatest reluctance and misgiving. The reader of that day probably found it hard, remote, unimaginative; its style repellent, its treatment unsystematic, its method abstract and passionless. Yet even in this clothing its strange mixture of audacity and diffidence, of independence and selflessness, has achieved, whether by attraction and repulsion. a not easily estimable influence on human thought and feeling and action."

✔   ✔   ✔

On Wages

Labor, like all other things which are purchased and sold, and which may be increased or diminished in quantity, has its natural and its market price. The natural price of labor is that price which is necessary to enable

153

the laborers, one with another, to subsist and to perpetuate their race, without either increase or diminution.

The power of the laborer to support himself, and the
family which may be necessary to keep up the number
of laborers, does not depend on the quantity of money
which he may receive for wages, but on the quantity of
food, necessaries, and conveniences become essential to
him from habit which that money will purchase. The
natural price of labor, therefore, depends on the price of
the food, necessaries, and conveniences required for the
support of the laborer and his family. With a rise in the
price of food and necessaries, the natural price of labor
will rise; with the fall in their price, the natural price of
labor will fall.

With the progress of society the natural price of labor
has always a tendency to rise, because one of the principal commodities by which its natural price is regulated
has a tendency to become dearer from the greater difficulty of producing it. As, however, the improvements in
agriculture, the discovery of new markets, whence pro-
visions may be imported, may for a time counteract the
tendency to a rise in the price of necessaries, and may
even occasion their natural price to fall, so will the same
causes produce the correspondent effects on the natural
price of labor.

The natural price of all commodities, excepting raw
produce and labor, has a tendency to fall in the progress
of wealth and population; for though, on one hand, they
are enhanced in real value, from the rise in the natural
price of the raw material of which they are made, this is
more than counterbalanced by the improvements in
machinery, by the better division and distribution of
labour, and by the increasing skill, both in science and
art, of the producers.

The market price of labor is the price which is really
paid for it, from the natural operation of the proportion
of the supply to the demand; labor is dear when it is
scarce and cheap when it is plentiful. However much
the market price of labor may deviate from its natural
price, it has, like commodities, a tendency to conform to
it.

It is when the market price of labor exceeds its natural

price that the condition of the laborer is flourishing and happy, that he has it in his power to command a greater proportion of the necessaries and enjoyments of life, and therefore to rear a healthy and numerous family. When, however, by the encouragement which high wages give to the increase of population, the number of laborers is increased, wages again fall to their natural price, and indeed from a reaction sometimes fall below it.

When the market price of labor is below its natural price, the condition of the laborers is most wretched: then poverty deprives them of those comforts which custom renders absolute necessaries. It is only after their privations have reduced their number, or the demand for labor has increased, that the market price of labor will rise to its natural price, and that the laborer will have the moderate comforts which the natural rate of wages will afford.

Notwithstanding the tendency of wages to conform to their natural rate, their market rate may, in an improving society, for an indefinite period, be constantly above it; for no sooner may the impulse which an increased capital gives to a new demand for labor be obeyed, than another increase of capital may produce the same effect; and thus, if the increase of capital be gradual and constant, the demand for labor may give a continued stimulus to an increase of people.

Capital is that part of the wealth of a country which is employed in production, and consists of food, clothing, tools, raw materials, machinery, etc., necessary to give effect to labor.

Capital may increase in quantity at the same time that its value rises. An addition may be made to the food and clothing of a country at the same time that more labor may be required to produce the additional quantity than before; in that case not only the quantity but the value of capital will rise.

Or capital may increase without its value increasing, and even while its value is actually diminishing; not only may an addition be made to the food and clothing of a country, but the addition may be made by the aid of machinery, without any increase, and even with an absolute diminution in the proportional quantity of

labor required to produce them. The quantity of capital
may increase, while neither the whole together, nor any
part of it singly, will have a greater value than before,
but may actually have a less.

In the first case, the natural price of labor, which
always depends on the price of food, clothing, and other
necessaries, will rise; in the second, it will remain
stationary or fall; but in both cases the market rate of
wages will rise, for in proportion to the increase of
capital will be the increase in the demand for labor; in
proportion to the work to be done will be the demand
for those who are to do it.

In both cases, too, the market price of labor will rise
above its natural price; and in both cases it will have a
tendency to conform to its natural price, but in the first
case this agreement will be most speedily effected. The
situation of the laborer will be improved, but not much
improved; for the increased price of food and necessaries
will absorb a large portion of his increased wages;
consequently a small supply of labor, or a trifling increase in the population, will soon reduce the market
price to the then increased natural price of labor.

In the second case, the condition of the laborer will
be very greatly improved; he will receive increased
money wages without having to pay any increased price,
and perhaps even a diminished price for the commodities
which he and his family consume; and it will not be till
after a great addition has been made to the population
that the market price of labor will again sink to its then
low and reduced natural price.

Thus, then, with every improvement of society, with
every increase in its capital, the market wages of labor
will rise; but the permanence of their rise will depend
on the question whether the natural price of labor has
also risen; and this again will depend on the rise in the
natural price of those necessaries on which the wages
of labor are expended.

It is not to be understood that the natural price of
labor, estimated even in food and necessaries, is absolutely fixed and constant. It varies at different times in
the same country, and very materially differs in different
countries. It essentially depends on the habits and

customs of the people. An English laborer would consider his wages under their natural rate, and too scanty to support a family, if they enabled him to purchase no other food than potatoes, and to live in no better habitation than a mud cabin; yet these moderate demands of nature are often deemed sufficient in countries where "man's life is cheap" and his wants easily satisfied. Many of the conveniences now enjoyed in an English cottage would have been thought luxuries at an earlier period of our history.

From manufactured commodities always falling and raw produce always rising, with the progress of society, such a disproportion in their relative value is at length created, that in rich countries a laborer, by the sacrifice of a very small quantity only of his food, is able to provide liberally for all his other wants.

Independently of the variations in the value of money, which necessarily effect money wages, but which we have here supposed to have no operation, as we have considered money to be uniformly of the same value, it appears then that wages are subject to a rise or fall from two causes:—

First, the supply and demand of laborers.

Secondly, the price of the commodities on which the wages of labor are expended.

In different stages of society, the accumulation of capital, or of the means of employing labor, is more or less rapid, and must in all cases depend on the productive powers of labor. The productive powers of labor are generally greatest when there is an abundance of fertile land: at such periods accumulation is often so rapid that laborers cannot be supplied with the same rapidity as capital.

It has been calculated that under favorable circumstances population may be doubled in twenty-five years; but under the same favorable circumstances the whole capital of a country might possibly be doubled in a shorter period. In that case, wages during the whole period would have a tendency to rise, because the demand for labor would increase still faster than the supply.

— Reading No. 14 —

MONTESQUIEU: *THE SPIRIT OF THE LAWS*

Charles Louis de Secondat, Baron de la Brède et de Montesquieu (1689-1755), a French philosophical historian of distinguished family, achieved enduring fame as the author of *The Spirit of the Laws*. A committee of friends, including Helvétius, read the manuscript and unanimously recommended that it not be published. It became one of the most important books ever written. A long essay of thirty-one tersely written parts in two volumes, it was, in essence, a keen analysis of political authority. In the words of George Saintsbury: "The real importance of the *Esprit des lois* is not that of a formal treatise on law, or even on polity. It is an assemblage of the most fertile, original and inspiriting views on legal and political subjects, put in language of singular suggestiveness and vigor, illustrated by examples which are always apt and luminous, permeated by the spirit of temperate and tolerant desire for human improvement and happiness, and almost unique in its entire freedom at once from doctrinism, from visionary enthusiasm, from egotism, and from an undue spirit of system." For Montesquieu no law is good or bad in itself. Those laws are good that are successful and that bring greater happiness to those for whom they are made; conversely, those laws are bad that fail, and bring about distress and disorder. The following extracts from the opening book illustrate Montesquieu's ideas on laws in general.

Of Laws in General

Laws, in their most general signification, are the necessary relations arising from the nature of things. In this sense all beings have their laws; the Deity His laws, the material world its laws, the intelligences superior to man their laws, the beasts their laws, man his laws.

They who assert that a blind fatality produced the various effects we behold in this world talk very absurdly; for can anything be more unreasonable than to pretend that a blind fatality could be productive of intelligent beings?

There is, then, a prime reason; and laws are the relations subsisting between it and different beings, and the relations of these to one another.

God is related to the universe, as Creator and Preserver; the laws by which He created all things are those by which He preserves them. He acts according to these rules, because He knows them; He knows them, because He made them; and He made them because they are in relation to His wisdom and power.

Since we observe that the world, though formed by the motion of matter, and void of understanding, subsists through so long a succession of ages, its motions must certainly be directed by invariable laws; and could we imagine another world, it must also have constant rules, or it would inevitably perish.

Thus the creation, which seems an arbitrary act, supposes laws as invariable as those of the fatality of the atheists. It would be absurd to say that the Creator might govern the world without those rules, since without them it could not subsist.

These rules are a fixed and invariable relation. In bodies moved, the motion is received, increased, diminished, or lost, according to the relations of the quantity of matter and velocity; each diversity is uniformity, each change is constancy. . . .

Man, as a physical being, is like other bodies governed by invariable laws. As an intelligent being, he incessantly transgresses the laws established by God, and changes

those of his own instituting. He is left to his private
direction, though a limited being, and subject, like all
finite intelligences, to ignorance and error: even in
imperfect knowledge he loses; and as a sensible creature,
he is hurried away by a thousand impetuous passions.
Such a being might every instant forget his Creator; God
has therefore reminded him of his duty by the laws of
religion. Such a being is liable every moment to forget
himself; philosophy has provided against this by the
laws of morality. Formed to live in society, he might
forget his fellow creatures; legislators have therefore by
political and civil laws confined him to his duty. . . .

As soon as man enters into a state of society he loses
the sense of his weakness; equality ceases, and then
commences the state of war.

Each particular society begins to feel its strength,
whence arises a state of war between different nations.
The individuals likewise of each society become sensible
of their force; hence the principal advantages of this
society they endeavor to convert to their own emolument,
which constitutes a state of war between individuals.

These two different kinds of states give rise to human
laws. Considered as inhabitants of so great a planet,
which necessarily contains a variety of nations, they have
laws relating to their mutual intercourse, which is what
we call the law of nations. As members of a society that
must be properly supported, they have laws relating to
the governors and the governed, and this we distinguish
by the name of politic law. They have also another
sort of laws, as they stand in relation to each other; by
which is understood civil law.

The law of nations is naturally founded on this
principle, that different nations ought in time of peace
to do one another all the good they can, and in time of
war as little injury as possible, without prejudicing their
real interests.

The object of war is victory; that of victory is conquest; and that of conquest preservation. From this and
the preceding principle all those rules are derived which
constitute the law of nations.

All countries have a law of nations, not excepting the
Iroquois themselves, though they devour their prisoners:

for they send and receive ambassadors, and understand the rights of war and peace. The mischief is that their law of nations is not founded on true principles.

Besides the law of nations relating to all societies, there is a polity or civil constitution for each particularly concerned. No society can subsist without a form of government. "The united strength of individuals," as Gravina (*Italian poet and jurist, 1664-1718*) well observes, "constitutes what we call the body politic."

The general force may be in the hands of a single person, or of many. Some think that Nature having established paternal authority, the most natural government was that of a single person. But the example of paternal authority proves nothing. For if the power of a father relates to a single government, that of brothers after the death of a father, and that of cousin-germans after the decease of brothers, refer to a government of many. The political power necessarily comprehends the union of several families.

Better is it to say that the government most conformable to Nature is that which best agrees with the humor and disposition of the people in whose favor it is established.

The strength of individuals cannot be united without a conjunction of their wills. "The conjunction of those wills," as Gravina again very justly observes, "is what we call the civil state."

Law in general is human reason, inasmuch as it governs all the inhabitants of the earth; the political and civil laws of each nation ought to be only the particular cases in which human reason is applied.

They should be adapted in such a manner to the people for whom they are framed that it should be a great chance if those of one nation suit another.

They should be in relation to the nature and principle of each government; whether they form it, as may be said of politic laws; or whether they support it, as in the case of civil institutions.

They should be in relation to the climate of each country, to the quality of its soil, to its situation and extent, to the principal occupation of the natives, whether husbandmen, huntsmen, or shepherds: they should have relation to the degree of liberty which the constitution will bear; to the religion of the inhabitants, to their inclinations, riches, numbers, commerce, manners, and customs. In fine, they have relations to each other, as also to their origin, to the intent of the legislator, and to the order of things on which they are established; in all of which different lights they ought to be considered.

These relations . . . all together constitute what I call the "Spirit of the Laws."

— Reading No. 15 —

JOHN MILTON: *AREOPAGITICA*

The rationalist belief in tolerance was expressed eloquently by John Milton (1608-1674) in his famed *Areopagitica* (1644). Its immediate occasion was an order of June, 1643, by which Parliament re-established the censorship of the press. In his protest Milton sought to show the absurdity and iniquity of this measure, but often he went beyond the immediate order and tried to prove that freedom of speech and action are not evils to be tolerated, but actually blessings that are essential to the life and happiness of any nation. "Give me the liberty," he writes, "to know, to utter, and to argue freely, according to conscience, above all liberties." Despite the exotic style, still marked by Latin influence, the *Areopagitica* is a magnificent contribution to human thought. It is, in the words of C. E. Vaughan, "an imperishable monument to the nobility of Milton's personal creed, an uncompromising plea for the rights of reason and of progress."

✓   ✓   ✓

I deny not, but that it is of greatest concernment in the Church and Commonwealth, to have a vigilant eye how books demean themselves as well as men; and thereafter to confine, imprison, and do sharpest justice on them as malefactors. For books are not absolutely dead things, but do contain a potency of life in them to be as active as that soul was whose progeny they are; nay, they do preserve as in a vial the purest efficacy and extraction of that living intellect that bred them. I know they are as lively, and as vigorously productive, as those fabulous dragon's teeth; and being sown up and down, may chance to spring up armed men. And yet, on the other hand, unless wariness be used, as good almost kill a man as kill a good book. Who kills a man kills a reasonable creature, God's image; but he who destroys a good book, kills reason itself, kills the image of God, as it were in the eye. Many a man lives a burden to the earth; but a good book is the precious life-blood of a master spirit, embalmed and treasured up on purpose to a life beyond life. 'Tis true, no age can restore a life, whereof perhaps there is not great loss; and revolutions of ages do not oft recover the loss of a rejected truth, for the want of which whole nations fare the worse.

We should be wary therefore what persecution we raise against the living labors of public men, how we spill that seasoned life of man, preserved and stored up in books; since we see a kind of homicide may be thus committed, sometimes a martyrdom, and if it extends to the whole impression, a kind of massacre; whereof the execution ends not in the slaying of an elemental life, but strikes at that ethereal and fifth essence, the breath of reason itself, slays an immortality rather than a life. . . .

Seeing . . . that those books, and those in great abundance, which are likeliest to taint both life and doctrine, cannot be suppressed without the fall of learning, and of all ability in disputation, and that these books of either sort are most and soonest catching to the learned, from whom to the common people whatever is heretical or dissolute may quickly be conveyed, and that evil manners are as perfectly learnt without books a thousand other ways which cannot be stopped, and evil doctrine not with books can propagate, except a teacher guide, which he might also do without writing, and so beyond prohibiting, I am not able to unfold, how this cautelous enterprise of licensing can be exempted from the number of vain and impossible attempts. And he who were pleasantly disposed could not well avoid to liken it to the exploit of that gallant man who thought to pound up the crows by shutting his park gate.

Besides another inconvenience, if learned men be the first receivers out of books and dispreaders both of vice and error, how shall the licensers themselves be confided in, unless we can confer upon them, or they assume to themselves above all others, in the land, the grace of infallibility and uncorruptedness? And again, if it be true that a wise man, like a good refiner, can gather gold out of the drossest volume, and that a fool will be a fool with the best book, yea or without book; there is no reason that we should deprive a wise man of any advantage to his wisdom, while we seek to restrain from a fool, that which being restrained will be no hindrance to his folly. For if there should be much exactness always used to keep that from him which is unfit for his reading, we should in the judgment of Aristotle not only, but of Solomon and of our Saviour, not vouchsafe him good precepts, and by consequence not willingly admit him to good books; as being certain that a wise man will make better use of an idle pamphlet, than a fool will do of sacred Scripture. . . .

If we think to regulate printing, thereby to rectify manners, we must regulate all recreations and pastimes, all that is delightful to man. No music must be heard, no song be set or sung, but what is grave and Doric. There must be licensing dancers, that no gesture, motion, or deportment be taught our youth but what by their allowance shall be thought honest; for such Plato was provided of; it will ask more than the work of twenty licensers to examine all the lutes, the violins, and the guitars in every house; they must not be suffered to prattle as they do, but must be licenses what they may say. And who shall silence all the airs and madrigals that whisper softness in chambers? The windows also, and the balconies must be thought on; there are shrewd books, with dangerous frontispieces, set to sale; who shall prohibit them, shall twenty licensers? The villages also must have their visitors to inquire what lectures the bagpipe and the rebeck reads, even to the ballatry and the gamut of every municipal fiddler, for these are the countryman's Arcadias and his Monte Mayors.

Next, what more national corruption, for which England hears ill abroad, than household gluttony: who shall be the rectors of our daily rioting? And what shall be done to inhibit the multitudes that frequent those houses where drunkenness is sold and harbored? Our garments also should be referred to the licensing of some more sober workmasters to see them out into a less wanton garb. Who shall regulate all the mixed conversation of our youth, male and female together, as is the fashion of this country? Who shall still appoint what shall be discoursed, what presumed, and no further? Lastly, who shall forbid and separate all idle resort, all evil company? These things will be, and must be; but how they shall be least hurtful, how least enticing, herein consists the grave and governing wisdom of a state. . . .

Lords and Commons of England, consider what Nation it is whereof ye are, and whereof ye are the governors: a Nation not slow and dull, but of a quick, ingenious and piercing spirit, acute to invent, subtle and sinewy to discourse, not beneath the reach of any point, the highest that human capacity can soar to. Therefore the studies of Learning in her deepest sciences have been so ancient and eminent among us, that writers of good antiquity and ablest judgment have been persuaded that even the school of Pythagoras and the Persian wisdom took beginning from the old philosophy of this island. And that wise and civil Roman, Julius Agricola, who governed once here for Caesar, preferred the natural wits of Britain before the laborious studies of the French. Nor is it for nothing that the grave and frugal Transylvanians send out yearly from as far as the mountainous borders of Russia, and beyond the Hercynian wilderness, not their youth, but their staid men, to learn our language and our theologic arts.

Yet that which is above all this, the favor and the love of Heaven, we have great argument to think in a peculiar manner propitious and propending towards us. Why else was this Nation chosen before any other, that out of her, as out of Sion, should be proclaimed and sounded forth the first tidings and trumpet of Reformation to all Europe? . . .

And as for regulating the Press, let no man think to

have the honor of advising ye better than yourselves have done in that Order published next before this, "that no book be Printed, unless the Printer's and the Author's name, or at least the Printer's, be registered." Those which otherwise come forth, if they be found mischievous and libellous, the fire and the executioner will be the timeliest and the most effectual remedy that man's prevention can use. For this authentic Spanish policy of licensing books, if I have said aught, will prove the most unlicensed book itself within a short while; and was the immediate image of a Star Chamber decree to that purpose made in those very times when that Court did the rest of her pious works, for which she is now fallen from the stars with Lucifer. . . .

This I know, that errors in a good government and in a bad are equally almost incident; for what Magistrate may not be misinformed, and much the sooner, if Liberty of Printing be reduced into the power of a few? But to redress willingly and speedily what hath been erred, and in highest authority to esteem a plain advertisement more than others have done a sumptuous bribe, is a virtue (honored Lords and Commons) answerable to your highest actions, and whereof none can participate but greatest and wisest men.

— Reading No. 16 —

ROUSSEAU: *THE SOCIAL CONTRACT*

The Social Contract, written by the Genevan philosopher Jean-Jacques Rousseau (1712-1778), is considered by many to be the most influential treatise on politics written in modern times. Published in 1762 under the title of *The Social Contract, or, Principles of Political Right,* the essay was a classic treatment of the contract theory of the state. Where Montesquieu started with laws and tried to find out what sort of men they made, Rousseau took man as the basis, and regards him as giving himself what laws he pleases. In other words, Rousseau sought to make the will of the members the base of every society. This extraordinary work, while including debatable premises and unreal hypotheses, became the literary inspiration of the French Revolution. It stimulated a host of imitators. It is the bible of contemporary politics and the major source of the doctrine of popular sovereignty. Rousseau's terms of the social contract were given in the following words.

↗   ↗   ↗

Man is born free, yet everywhere he is in chains. One thinks himself the master of others, and still remains a greater slave than they. How did this change come about? I do not really know. What can make it legitimate? I think I can answer that question.

If I took into account only force, as well as the effects derived from it, I should say: "So long as a people is compelled to obey, and obeys, it does well; as soon as it can shake off the yoke, and does shake it off, it does still better, for regaining its liberty by the same right as took it away either it is justified in resuming it, or there was no justification for those who took it away." The social order is a sacred right which is the basis of all other rights. Nevertheless, this right does not come from one nature, and must be founded therefore on convention. . . .

I suppose men to have reached the point at which the obstacles in the way of their preservation in the state of nature show their power of resistance to be greater than the resources of each individual for his maintenance in that state. That condition of primitiveness can then subsist no longer. The human race would perish unless it changed its manner of existence.

But, since men cannot engender new forces, but only unite and direct those which already exist, they have no other means of preserving themselves than by the formation, in aggregation, of a sum of forces great enough to overcome the resistance. These they must bring into play by means of a single motive power, and cause to act in concert.

This sum of forces can arise only when several persons come together, but since the force and liberty of each man are the chief instruments of his self-preservation, how can he pledge them without harm to his own interests, and without neglecting the care which he owes to himself? This difficulty, in so far as it relates to my present subject, may be stated in these terms:

"The problem is to find a form of association that will defend and protect with the whole common force the person and property of each associate, and in which each, while uniting himself with all, may still obey himself alone, and still remain as free as before." This is the basic problem for which the *Social Contract* gives the solution.

The clauses of this contract are so determined by the nature of the act that the least modification would make them vain and without effect, so that, although they have perhaps never formally been set forth, they are everywhere the same and everywhere tacitly admitted and recognized, until, on the violation of the social compact,

each regains his original rights and resumes his natural
liberty, while he loses the conventional liberty in favor
of those who renounced it.

When properly understood these clauses may be reduced to one: the total alienation of each associate, in
common with all his rights, to the whole community.
This is because in the first place, since each gives himself absolutely, the conditions are the same for all. This
being so, no one has any interest in making them bur-
densome to others.

In addition, the alienation being without reserve, the
union is as perfect as it can possibly be, and no associate
has anything more to demand; for, if the individual
retained certain rights, as there would be no common
superior to decide between them and the public, each,
being on one point his own judge, would ask to be so
on all. The state of nature would thus continue, and the
association would necessarily become inoperative and
tyrannical.

Finally, each individual, in giving himself to all, gives
himself to nobody. Since there is no associate over
whom he does not acquire the same right as he yields
others over himself, he gains an equivalent for everything he loses, and an increase of force for the preservation of what he has.

If we discard from the social compact what is not
essential, we shall find that it reduces itself to the following terms:

*"Each of us puts his person and all his power in
common under the supreme direction of the general will
and, in our corporate capacity, we received each member as an indivisible part of the whole."*

This act of association immediately, in place of the
individual personality of each contracting party, creates
a moral and collective body, composed of as many members as the assembly contains votes, and receiving from
this act its unity, its common identity, its life, and its
will. This public person, so formed by the union of all
other persons, formerly took the name of *city,* and now
takes that of *Republic* or *body politic.* It is called by its
members *State* when passive, *Sovereign* when active, and
Power when compared with others like itself. Those who

are associated in it take collectively the name of *people,* and severally are called *citizens,* who share in the sovereign power, and *subjects,* since they are under the laws of the State. These terms are often confused and taken one from another; it is enough to know how to distinguish them when they are used with precision. . . .

In order that the social compact may not be an empty formula, it tacitly includes the undertaking, which in itself gives force to the rest, that whoever refuses to obey the general will shall be compelled to do so by the whole body. This means nothing less than that he will be forced to be free, for this is the condition which, in giving each citizen to the country, secures him against all personal dependence. In this lies the key to the working of the political machine. This alone makes legitimate civil undertakings, which, without it, would be quite absurd, tyrannical, and open to the most frightful abuses.

The passage from the state of nature to civil state produces a most remarkable change in man, in substituting justice for instinct in his conduct, and in giving his actions the sense of morality which they formerly did not possess. It is then only, when the voice of duty takes the place of physical impulses and the right of appetite, that man, who to this point had considered only himself, finds that he is forced to act on somewhat different principles, and to consult his reason before listening to his inclinations. Although he deprives himself of some advantages which he had gotten from nature, he gains others so great, his faculties are so stimulated and developed, his ideas so extended, his feelings so ennobled, and his soul so much uplifted, that, if the abuses of this new condition often degrade him below that which he left, he would be bound continually to bless the happy moment which took him from it forever, and, instead of being a stupid and unimaginative animal, made him an intelligent human being and man.

Let us state the account in terms easily understood. What man loses by the social contract is his natural liberty and an unlimited right to everything he tries to get and succeeds in getting. What he gains is civil liberty and the ownership of all he possesses. If we are to avoid errors in weighing one against the other, we must make a clear distinction between *natural liberty*, which is bounded only by the strength of the individual, and *civil liberty*, which remains under the limit of the general will; and *possession*, which is simply the effect of force or the right of the first occupier, and *property*, which can be based only on a positive title.

Over and above all this we might add to what man acquires in the civil state—*moral liberty* which alone makes him truly the master of himself, since the mere impulse of appetite is slavery, while obedience to a law which we prescribe for ourselves is liberty.

JEFFERSON: *A LETTER ON DEMOCRACY*

In France, liberty, equality, and fraternity were theories, but in America they were indigenous facts, natural to farmer-pioneers who lived in freedom from governmental interference. Thomas Jefferson (1743-1826), who was familiar with the basic elements of French and British rationalist thought, merely adapted them to American conditions. An egalitarian democrat, he believed in the people. He fought for freedom—from the British crown, from religious disabilities, from inequalities of wealth, and from the landed aristocracy. He was under the influence of Helvétius, Locke, and Rousseau when he wrote into the Declaration of Independence the statement: "We hold these truths to be self-evident, That all men are created equal." In the following letter to Dupont de Nemours, dated April 24, 1816, Jefferson summarized his conception of democratic government and emphasized his abiding faith in the wisdom of the people.

✓   ✓   ✓

TO MONSIEUR DUPONT DE NEMOURS

POPLAR FOREST, April 24, 1816

I received, my dear friend, your letter covering the Constitution of your Equinoctial republics, just as I was setting out for this place. I brought it with me, and have read it with great satisfaction. I suppose it well formed for those for whom it was intended, and the excellence of every government is its adaptation to the state of those to be governed by it. For us it would not do. Distinguishing between the structure of the government and the moral principles on which you prescribe its administration, with the latter we concur cordially, with the former we should not.

We of the United States, you know, are constitutionally and conscientiously democrats. We consider society as one of the natural wants with which man has been created; that he has been endowed with faculties and qualities to effect its satisfaction by concurrence of others having the same want; that when, by the exercise of these faculties, he has procured a state of society, it is one of his acquisitions which he has a right to regulate and control, jointly indeed with all those who have concurred in the procurement, whom he cannot exclude from its use or direction more than they him. We think experience has proved it safer, for the mass of individuals composing the society, to reserve to themselves personally the exercise of all rightful powers to which they are competent, and to delegate those to which they are not competent to deputies named, and removable for unfaithful conduct, by themselves immediately.

Hence, with us, the people (by which is meant the mass of individuals composing the society) being competent to judge of the facts occurring in ordinary life, they have retained the functions of judges of facts, under the name of jurors; but being unqualified for the management of affairs requiring intelligence above the common level, yet competent judges of human character, they chose, for their management, representatives, some by themselves immediately, others by electors chosen by themselves. Thus our President is chosen by ourselves, directly in *practice,* for we vote for A as elector only on the condition that he will vote for B, our representatives by ourselves immediately, our Senate and judges of law through electors chosen by ourselves. And we believe that this proximate choice and power of removal is the best security which experience has sanctioned for ensuring an honest conduct in the functionaries of society. . . .

I acknowledge myself strong in affection to our own form, yet both of us act and think from the same motive, we both consider the people as our children, and love them with parental affection. But you love them as infants whom you are afraid to trust without nurses; and I as adults whom I freely leave to self-government. And you are right in the case referred to you; my criticism being built on a state of society not under your contemplation. It is, in fact, like a critic on Homer by the laws of the Drama.

But when we come to the moral principles on which the government is to be administered, we come to what is proper for all conditions of society. I meet you there in all the benevolence and rectitude of your native character; and I love myself always most where I concur most with you. Liberty, truth, probity, honor, are declared to be the four cardinal principles of your society. I believe with you that morality, compassion, generosity, are innate elements of the human constitution; that there exists a right independent of force; that a right to property is founded in our natural wants, in the means with which we are endowed to satisfy these wants, and the right to what we acquire by those means without violating the similar rights of other sensible beings; that no one has a right to obstruct another, exercising his faculties innocently for the relief of sensibilities made a part of his nature; that justice is the fundamental law of society; that the majority, oppressing an individual, is guilty of a crime, abuses its strength, and by acting on the law of the strongest, breaks up the foundations of society; that action by the citizens in person, in affairs within their reach and competence, and in all others by representatives, chosen immediately, and removable by themselves, constitutes the essence of a republic; that all governments are more or less republican in proportion as this principle enters more or less into their composition; and that a government by representation is capable of extension over a greater surface of country than one of any other form. These, my friend, are the essentials in which you and I agree; however, in our zeal for their maintenance, we may be perplexed and divaricate, as to the structure of society most likely to secure them.

In the Constitution of Spain, as proposed by the late Cortes, there was a principle entirely new to me, and not noticed in yours, that no person, born after that day, should ever acquire the rights of citizenship until he could read and write. It is impossible sufficiently to estimate the wisdom of this provision. Of all those which have been thought of for securing fidelity in the administration of government, constant ralliance to the principles of the Constitution, and progressive amendments with the progressive advances of the human mind, or changes in human affairs, it is the most effectual. Enlighten the people generally, and tyranny and oppressions of body and mind will vanish like evil spirits at the dawn of day. Although I do not, with some enthusiasts, believe that the human condition will ever advance to such a state of perfection as that there shall no longer be pain or vice in the world, yet I believe it is susceptible of much improvement, and most of all, in matters of government and religion; and that the diffusion of knowledge among the people is to be the instrument by which it is to be effected. The Constitution of the Cortes had defects enough; but when I saw in it this amendatory provision, I was satisfied all would come right in time, under its salutary operation. No people have more need of a similar provision than those for whom you have felt so much interest.

No mortal wishes them more success than I do. But if what I have heard of the ignorance and bigotry of the mass be true, I doubt their capacity to understand and support a free government; and fear that their emancipation from the foreign tyranny of Spain, will result in a military despotism at home. Palacios may be great; others may be great; but it is the multitude which possesses force; and wisdom must yield to that. For such a condition of society, the Constitution you have devised is probably the best imaginable. It is certainly calculated to solicit the best talents; although perhaps not well guarded against the egoism of its functionaries. But that egoism will be light in comparison with the pressures of a military despot, and his army of Janissaries. Like

Solon to the Athenians, you have given to your Colum-
bians, not the best possible government, but the best that
they can bear. By-the-bye, I wish you had called them
the Columbian republics, to distinguish them from our
American republics. Theirs would be the more honorable
name, and they best entitled to it; for Columbus discovered their continent, but never saw ours.

To them liberty and happiness; to you the need of
wisdom and goodness in teaching them how to attain
them, with the affectionate respect and friendship of
Th.J.

SOURCES FOR SELECTED READINGS

1. Bacon, Francis, *Novum Organum, or True Suggestions for the Interpretation of Nature* (London, 1844), pp. 9-20.
2. Descartes, René, *Discourse on the Method of Rightly Conducting the Reason and Seeking Truth in the Sciences,* trans. by John Veitch (London, 1907), pp. 17-23.
3. Newton, Sir Isaac, *Mathematical Principles of Natural Philosophy and System of the World,* trans. by Andrew Motte (London, 1729) from the original edition, *Philosophiae Naturalis Principia Mathematica* (London, 1687), Introduction, *passim.*
4. Spinoza, Baruch, *The Ethics* (Amsterdam, 1677), Part I, *passim.*
5. Voltaire, *Philosophical Dictionary* (Boston, 1856), II, pp. 132, 344, 356-57, 360 ff. Adapted.
6. Butler, Bishop Joseph, *The Analogy of Religion, Natural and Revealed, to the Constitution and Course of Nature* (Cincinnati, 1847), pp. 313-14, 320-21.
7. Hobbes, Thomas, *Leviathan, or the Matter, Form, and Power of a Commonwealth, Ecclesiastical and Civil* (London, 1651), Part 2, chap. 17.
8. Locke, John, *An Essay Concerning Human Understanding* (20th ed., London, 1796), Book I, pp. 1-5; Book 2, pp. 77-79.
9. Berkeley, George, *The Principles of Human Knowledge, a Treatise on the Nature of the Material Substance and Its Relation to the Absolute* (London, 1710), chaps. 1, 2, sects. 1, 2, 3, 4, 5, 8, 22.
10. Condorcet, Jean Antoine Nicolas Caritat, Marquis de, *Outlines of an Historical View of the Progress of the Human Mind* (London, 1795), pp. 366-72.
11. Smith, Adam, *An Inquiry into the Nature and*

Causes of the Wealth of Nations (London, 1776), Book 4, chap. 1, *passim.*

12. Malthus, Thomas Robert, *An Essay on the Principle of Population or, A View of its Past and Present Effects on Human Happiness; with an Inquiry into our Prospects Respecting the Future Removal or Mitigation of the Evils which it Occasions* (London, 1826), pp. 1-11, 12, 15.

13. Ricardo, David, *The Principles of Political Economy and Taxation* (London, 1819), chap. 5, pp. 85-93.

14. Montesquieu, Charles Louis de Secondat, Baron de la Brède et de, *The Spirit of the Laws,* trans. from the French by Mr. Nugent (London, 1858), Book I, pp. 1-2, 4, 7-9.

15. Milton, John, *Areopagitica, A Speech for the Liberty of Unlicensed Printing, to the Parliament of England* (London, 1644), pp. 34-79, *passim.*

16. Rousseau, Jean Jacques, *The Social Contract, or, Principles of Political Right* (Paris, 1762), Book I, chaps. 1, 6, 8, *passim.*

17. Jefferson, Thomas, *Writings* (Washington, 1903), XIV, pp. 487-93.

A SHORT BIBLIOGRAPHY

Becker, Carl, *The Heavenly City of the Eighteenth-Century Philosophers* (New Haven, 1932).

Brinton, Crane, *Ideas and Men* (New York, 1950).

Frankel, Charles, *The Faith of Reason* (New York, 1948).

Hearnshaw, F. J. C., ed., *The Social and Political Ideas of Some Great French Thinkers of the Age of Reason* (London, 1930).

Hibben, J. G., *The Philosophy of the Enlightenment* (New York, 1910).

Laski, Harold, *Political Thought in England from Locke to Bentham* (New York, 1920).

Lovejoy, A. O., *The Great Chain of Being* (Cambridge, Mass., 1942).

Martin, Kingsley, *French Liberal Thought in the Eighteenth Century* (Boston, 1929).

Morley, John, *Diderot and the Encyclopedists* (London, 1914).

Randall, J. H., Jr., *The Making of the Modern Mind* (Boston, 1940).

Ritchie, D. G., *Natural Rights* (3rd ed., London, 1916).

Robertson, J. M., *A Short History of Free Thought* (2 vols., London, 1915).

Stephen, Leslie, *History of English Thought in the Eighteenth Century* (New York, 1902).

Willey, Basil, *The Eighteenth-Century Background* (New York, 1941).

Wright, B. F., *American Interpretations of Natural Law* (Cambridge, Mass., 1931).

INDEX

VAN NOSTRAND REINHOLD ANVIL BOOKS